WENSLEY CLARKSON is an investigative journalist who has written numerous non-fiction books, including best-selling true crime classics about three of America's most notorious serial killers. His books have sold more than a million copies in eighteen countries worldwide.

GANGS

OF BRITAIN

THE GRIPPING TRUE STORIES
OF THE FACES WHO RUN BRITAIN'S
ORGANISED CRIME

WENSLEY CLARKSON

JOHN BLAKE

Published by John Blake Publishing Ltd,
3 Bramber Court, 2 Bramber Road,
London W14 9PB, England

www.johnblakepublishing.co.uk

www.facebook.com/johnblakebooks ⬛
twitter.com/jblakebooks ⬛

First published in paperback in 2008

ISBN: 978 1 84454 518 6

British Library Cataloguing-in-Publication Data:

A catalogue record for this book is available from the British Library.

Design by www.envydesign.co.uk

Printed in Great Britain by CPI Group (UK) Ltd

9 10

Papers used by John Blake Publishing are natural, recyclable products made
from wood grown in sustainable forests. The manufacturing processes conform to
the environmental regulations of the country of origin.

Every attempt has been made to contact the relevant copyright-holders,
but some were unobtainable. We would be grateful if the appropriate people
could contact us.

CONTENTS

PROLOGUE

Organised crime in Britain makes the gangsters you are about to read about more than £10 billion a year. The New Labour Government has even fingered a 'dirty dozen' kingpins of crime with the aim of freezing all their assets. Any companies helping known villains will face multi-million-pound fines and other penalties.

Many of these names are legendary faces in global drug-smuggling cartels yet they continue to live openly inside Britain. And they haven't so far lost a penny in this so-called crackdown on their finances.

Successive Home Secretaries have reckoned that targeting businesses and individuals linked to these supergangsters will smoke them out. He must be living in cloud-cuckoo land. The names that have been passed on to the Government by the police are villains allegedly being chased by teams of investigators and tax officials planning to end their lives of crime. If that's the case why are they still out there on Britain's streets making millions?

Most of the gangsters you'll read about in this book are breaking the law big time without much interference. The Prime Minister and his team may have vowed to strip them of their assets in a drive to prove to the rest of the country that crime doesn't pay, but there's little sign of it yet. And remember, the then Home Secretary Jack Straw made his first pledge about breaking the gangsters back in 1998.

Straw vowed that the police would be allowed to seize assets if they could prove 'on the balance of probability' that the targets were living off the proceeds of their crimes. The Old Bill pushed for this power to grab dirty money from the bank accounts of major players in the most lucrative areas of crime, such as drugs, money laundering, counterfeiting, smuggling and computer fraud. But the law's been tearing their hair out ever since trying to confiscate cash from gangsters but finding it virtually impossible to prove anything 'beyond reasonable doubt'.

Roy Penrose, head of the Yard's elite National Crime Squad, insisted some years back, 'We are into tracking big business. The people involved often don't hide their wealth under a bushel, the natural thing to do is flaunt it – especially the ladies of the family. Profit is the only thing that drives these people. The idea of losing their £3 million pad, cars, jewellery and furs is not attractive. One of the impediments to the successful removal of the benefits or assets is the need at the moment to prove beyond reasonable doubt the offence. The civil balance of probabilities turns on the property. They would have to demonstrate it was acquired lawfully, with a full audit trail.'

Despite such pledges from the law and order brigade, more than 500 of Britain's top crime gangs are trafficking in narcotics worth at least £10 billion a year. The National Criminal Intelligence Service study into the nation's gangsters showed that, of 938 groups examined, more than 60% dealt in puff, half in Charlie and a similar number in heroin, and about 40% in so-called synthetic drugs, such as ecstasy. But because coke costs 10 to 20% more here in Britain than anywhere in Europe, the big firms have been doing most of their business in this country. A lot of them call it the gold rush. Many are making millions EVERY WEEK.

Most synthetic drugs are smuggled from the Netherlands and Belgium into London and Liverpool and distributed nationally. Businesses such as gyms and health clubs provide much safer cover for drug cartels selling cocaine, ecstasy and amphetamines than in the old days when nightclubs and boozers were the most popular legit cover for the huge amounts of cash flooding in.

Robbery, blagging as it's known in the trade, comes a long way down the pecking order these days. Three types of robbery were examined in a survey back in 1999: the well-planned attack by pros using firearms and violence which netted an estimated £2.5 million; attacks on couriers and vehicles by semi-pros, usually armed, got away with about £5.5 million; and the opportunists, who made £500,000. Only £1 million was recovered from a total of almost £10 million. Firearms were used in 220 attacks and 103 people were injured. In all there were nearly 500 attacks on security vans and couriers and about half were successful.

The big boys decided long ago that it's much smarter to put money into a drugs deal than dirty your hands by going across the pavement, as they used to do back in the days when John

Thaw and Dennis Waterman were screeching around London in their Granada having gun battles with armed blaggers on ITV's *The Sweeney*.

So it's easy to see why drugs provide gangsters with the biggest money they've ever known. The other old crimes of extortion and prostitution don't mean squirt compared to the profits of drug deals. Hard drugs like heroin and cocaine rule the market. More heroin was seized in Britain in recent years than any other European country. Opium production worldwide is running at record levels and imports into Britain are higher than ever. Customs reckon on seizing a ton of Charlie every year, but it's only a small fraction of what is getting through. Buying coke wholesale from Colombian cartels costs around £1,500 a kilo. The same drug cut and sold in London will fetch more than £100,000 a kilo. As they say, it's the gold rush all over again.

Ecstasy, bought wholesale in Holland for £6,000 a thousand tablets, sells in nightclubs across the country for as much as £25 a tablet. Cannabis, the most widely used drug of all, can be bought for £100 a kilo in the West Indies. In London it will sell for more than £2,000.

The cozzers reckon at least three London gangs are each making over £20 million a year from distributing drugs. That cash is then laundered through re-investment in restaurants, clubs and 'car fronts' – open-air used-motor lots are still one of the most popular ways to launder drugs money. The top faces also dip in and out of property deals, often working through legit nominees. One well-known London property dealer who owed £600,000 to a gangster was shot dead after failing to come up with the readies owed on a deal.

But all this silly money floating around has meant the number of shootings has rocketed in recent years. Illegal guns have become a sub-industry throughout gangsterdom. The most powerful faces have tasty collections of shooters including some of the most lethal weapons on the market. Machine pistols have become in-style items for the leading hard men in the same way that Gucci handbags have for their old ladies.

Underworld armourers operate lease-back schemes for guns to the smaller firms. Typically, a piece can be rented for a day at £250, or bought for £500. At least two of the best-known armourers in the London underworld in recent years have been ex-policemen.

Another little-known source of income for the big name gangsters is the trade in counterfeit currency. It's a very nifty sideline. A lot of villains have been swift to pick up on this. Recently, Barclays Bank intercepted £1.7 million worth of fake money. And they reckon more than £200 million in forged notes is floating around at any one time.

In the East End they still reckon that when the Krays were banged up the local crime rate doubled overnight because, whatever the twins might have been up to, their presence discouraged the small-timers. Truth is that the old-style gangsters of the Fifties and Sixties were a very different bunch from today's organised criminals. In those days, the big names were outlaws, of course, but they were seen as a stablising influence within their communities. Their power inspired respect, not just among rival villains but among small-time crooks who might otherwise have been tempted to prey on people on the manor. In South London, the Richardson brothers ruled with an iron hand. 'No one would dare mug an old lady on Charlie Richardson's manor,' one old-timer observed.

In Soho in the Fifties, the Maltese ran illegal gambling and prostitution. The Krays' speciality was extortion. The Richardsons were more sophisticated, although it was the infamous 'torture' episode – in which some rival villains were subjected to a bit of outrageous physical abuse – that put Charlie Richardson in jail for 25 years. Yet, as Charlie himself once pointed out, his victims were all other gangsters.

The old-timers were high profile and far less subterranean than the heavy characters around today. The Krays went to first nights, cultivating sporting and West End stars. In their heyday in the early Sixties they were often seen with some of the most glamorous people in London.

Today's godfathers stay in the shadows. Few really know them and, unlike their more colourful predecessors, no one wants to know them …

THE TENTACLES OF CRIME

I first got involved with the shady world of gangsters when I was working on a book about roadrage killer and underworld kingpin Kenny Noye. At the time, I hardly knew Noye's manor; an area that ran from the old docklands of Bermondsey south east through London and into deepest Kent. It's a patch known to local law enforcement as the 'Wild West'. 'What goes in there doesn't always come out,' says one veteran thief taker.

So when I tracked down some real-life villains for this book I wasn't so surprised when they painted an extraordinary picture of a society within a society where criminals and police exist in their own world with their own rules. Hundreds of professional hits are carried out each year in the name of these gangsters. It's chilling to think that such crimes are committed in Britain today, supposedly one of the most law-abiding countries in the world.

Many of the gangsters featured here live and thrive on the same sort of streets and supposedly respectable suburbs in which most 'normal' people live. In *Gangs of Britain*, I have tried to take the reader on an authentic, nail-biting, roller-coaster ride through the full, face-on brutality of Britain's underworld in the 21st century.

All roads in certain big cities lead to this subculture; even the appalling murder of black teenager Stephen Lawrence had a link to gangsters because the father of one of the suspects was an associate of Kenny Noye. During my travels I discovered that Noye had made a phone call from inside prison that allegedly enabled those suspects to walk out of a police station just hours after being arrested. The tentacles of master criminals stretch far beyond anything you could imagine.

As one retired detective told me, 'There are outlaws in Britain who are a law unto themselves. If they've got a problem with the police there's always someone they can call to sort things out.'

Today, drug lords rule most of the important manors. Their runners supply coke, puff and E to hundreds of thousands of drug users every week while they retreat to their million-pound detached mansions in the countryside. Ask any copper and he'll tell you it's true. In the Seventies and early Eighties highly professional teams of armed robbers ruled the underworld. But they soon realised that going across the pavement was a far riskier enterprise than putting 50 grand up for a drug deal that often guaranteed a return of 10 times that figure.

Numerous criminals have told me about the hitmen now constantly in demand for their specialised work. 'All the robbers of the Seventies are now dealing drugs big time. We're talkin' about millions of quid changin' hands every week. That means the rotten apples 'ave to be dealt with. There's no shortage of work for a decent shootist,' one retired cannabis smuggler told me.

He introduced me to a hitman we shall call 'Jake', a charming, charismatic man who at no time made me feel in danger. He assured me his only targets were other criminals. He had a wife, two kids, a house in the countryside and all the same problems as the rest of us. I've kept in touch with Jake and he enjoys the kick of being featured in a book, even though only his closest criminal associates would recognise him. He reckons it'll bring him even more respect on the manor.

In many ways I broke the writer's golden rule of getting too close to some of my subjects in *Gangs of Britain*. I had a few threats from the family of one well-known criminal when they thought I was pushing my luck in the name of research. It ended with a sinister phone call telling me that, 'We know where your kids go to school.' But that was it, thank God. Mind you, as another more friendly villain told me months later, 'If they'd really been after your kids they would hardly have bothered to tell you first, would they?'

Not everyone I've written about in *Gangs of Britain* is all bad. They can be funny and even kind and I tried to portray every aspect of their lives rather than just the predictable hardman mode. Many of them are smart survivors doing what they know best.

Sure, if you spend 340 nights a year ducking and diving around the mean streets you start to see the world differently from other people. You learn to survive by your instincts; you don't trust many people; you don't make light conversation because loose lips can sink ships; you spend each day thinking that your world may be shut down by a sharp-eyed policeman or a sneaky grass; you devise ways and means of keeping ahead of the game. Many of these criminals are undoubtedly trapped in their own little world, but then aren't the rest of us as well?

WENSLEY CLARKSON

2008

MEN ON A
MISSION

HOUNSLOW, WEST LONDON, 6.25AM,
26 NOVEMBER 1983

Only CCTV cameras and spotlights mounted on the walls of Unit 7, a steel and brick-built box on a scruffy trading estate near Heathrow Airport, caught the attention of curious onlookers. But when the huge orange-and-white armoured shutter doors rolled open the building's real purpose was revealed. Chunky dark-blue Brink's-Mat vans, with barred and tinted black windows, came and went from the well-protected loading bay day and night. Unit 7 wasn't Fort Knox or the Bank of England, but it did hold one of Britain's biggest safes, used to store currency, precious metals and other high-risk consignments often *en route* for Heathrow Airport.

Saturday, 26 November 1983, was pitch black and icy cold as a new early morning shift of workers waited outside, kicking their heels as they blew clouds of mist, waiting for 6.30am to arrive. That was when an automatic timer neutralised the high-tech alarm system, allowing the keys to be inserted without triggering flashing lights, bells and alarms linked with the local police station and other security companies.

Four guards pulled up and greeted each other. A fifth one was late and still hadn't arrived when the man who would supervise the day's work drove up. This so-called 'keyman' entered the unit alone, locking the door behind him and leaving the crew outside while he collected another key which shut down the alarm system covering the perimeter walls and windows. The four guards made their way to the rest room to take off their coats. One of them paused briefly to switch on the radio room aerials and the CCTV cameras before joining his mates.

Just then, the doorbell rang. It was the missing guard. He was ten minutes late. The guards heard the keyman go downstairs to let him in. He said he'd overslept, then, mumbling something about having to use the toilet, he disappeared downstairs again.

It was by now 6.40am.

'Get on the floor or you're fuckin' dead.'

A masked man filling the doorway of the rest area spat out the words in a heavy Cockney accent. He aimed his 9mm Browning automatic straight at the guards. Three of them dived for cover.

The armed blagger was white, about 5ft 8in tall and clean shaven, wearing a trilby and a dark car coat or anorak over a black blazer, black trousers and a black tie. He had on a yellow balaclava hitched up to cover all but his eyes.

For a second or two nothing happened, then the gunman jerked his gun arm upwards and, with a silver blazer button glinting in the light, smashed the shooter down on the head of one guard who hadn't gone to the floor quickly enough. Then he beckoned through the open door to someone waiting outside, and at least three more robbers stormed into the room.

'Lie still and be quiet,' ordered the original blagger, as his henchmen started yanking the guards' arms behind their backs and handcuffing them, then locking their legs together at the shins with heavy-duty masking tape. Cloth bags with strings were then pulled down over the guard's heads and fastened around their necks.

One guard saw enough of the main blagger to spot the herring-bone pattern of his tweed hat and the crispness of his starched white shirt. He even noticed a lock of fair hair sticking out from the balaclava as one of the bags was dropped over his head. Keys and watches were snatched from the guards.

Then another voice spat out, 'Get that radio tuned in. If you hear anythin', tell us.' This geezer was the boss. A radio crackled through frequencies until it tuned into a Met Police wavelength. No alarm calls had been made.

Then the 'keyman' felt his shirt pulled up to his chin and a hand tugging violently at his waistband. 'Breathe in deeply or I'll cut you.' Just then a knife sliced through his belted jeans from the buckle to the crutch. A rag was waved under his nose.

'Do you recognise that smell?'

It was unmistakable. The next instant he felt petrol stinging his tackle.

'Do as I fuckin' say, or I'll put a match to the petrol and a bullet through your fuckin' head. I know where you live. You live in a flat in Ruislip High Street above a TV rental shop. We've been watching you for nine months and settin' this up for twelve. Now, let's get on with it. You've got two numbers.'

It was all over in moments and the alarms were neutralised. The team was in. Inside Unit 7's vault the blaggers found a carpet of drab grey containers, no bigger than shoeboxes, bound with metal straps and labelled with handwritten identification codes. There were sixty boxes, containing 2,670 kilos of gold worth £26,369,778. There were also hundreds of thousands of quid in used banknotes locked in three safes. One pouch contained traveller's cheques worth $250,000. In the other was a stash of polished and rough diamonds worth at least 100 grand.

The atmosphere was buzzing as the team moved the gold out to the side of the loading bay and into their waiting vans. Sure, they'd expected riches but nothing like this. The Brink's-Mat robbery, ruthless in its conception and brilliant in its execution, had just landed them the biggest haul in British criminal history, a caper the tabloids soon labelled 'The Crime of the Century'.

Within 48 hours, Lloyds of London announced they'd pay two million quid for information leading to the return of the Brink's-Mat gold, which had already leapt in value by more than twenty pounds an ounce in the hours since the blagging.

The police soon narrowed down their list of suspects to some of the most notorious gangsters in and around London. They had two folders, each containing twelve photographs of the main men. Amongst those mugshots were a number of the faces you will read about in this book. Many of them were never caught, and most of those tens of millions of pounds have been reinvested in everything from cocaine and ecstasy shipments to brothels and a handful of major blaggings.

'Brink's-Mat made the names and fortunes of many of today's most ruthless gangsters,' says one who should know. 'It's the stuff of legends ...'

CHAPTER
1

THE 'A TEAM'

**'I didn't argue with them.
I didn't want any aggro.'**

**LONDON CLUB OWNER LEANED
ON BY THE ADAMS FAMILY.**

THE PRINCE ALFRED PUB, HUNTINGDON STREET, ISLINGTON, NORTH LONDON, 2 JANUARY 1990.

Patrick 'Patsy' Adams, tall, well-built, debonair master operator strode into the Prince Alfred – known to local faces as 'the quiet house' – in a deliberate wind-up right slap bang on the opposition's home turf. The Reilly gang fell for it hook, line and sinker.

Tensions between the two families had reached boiling point on New Year's Day, 1990, when one of the A-Team's lieutenants dissed George Reilly in front of his wife on a nearby Islington Street. Reilly was so narked he rushed home, grabbed a shooter and came back looking for the Adamses' henchman, who sought refuge in a nearby carpet shop. People scattered as Reilly took potshots from the street below. By a stroke of luck, no one was hit.

So when Patsy Adams strode into 'the quiet house' the next evening he knew what to expect. Word was quickly relayed to the Reillys, who dispatched a four-man unit of armed soldiers in a red BMW. As the Beemer turned down Huntingdon Street towards the Prince Alfred it drove right into Patsy Adams's trap. His team, carrying shotguns and pistols, were waiting at a junction in two cars and peppered the BMW with bullets.

Residents in the surrounding Victorian terraced houses dived for cover as the red Beemer reversed out of trouble at high speed, all guns blazing. Shots sprayed the pavement and people's garden walls, chipping brick work and ricocheting in all directions. Somehow, none of the home owners or the shooters in the Beemer were hit, but the sheer audacity of this wild-west-style shoot-out really got up the nose of the local Old Bill. They wanted to nail the A-Team before the streets of North London were turned into a 'no go' area for law-abiding citizens.

The police quickly traced the bullet-riddled red Beemer to club owner John Reilly, who was later jailed for 30 months at the Old Bailey after pleading guilty to violent conduct. But he and every other face involved in the legendary gun battle of Huntingdon Street have never openly admitted what really happened. Not surprisingly, the judge at John Reilly's trial described the Adamses as 'a group of first division criminals'.

The activities of the Adams family are notorious. Born and bred in Islington, North London, it's reckoned they're worth upwards of £100 million, making them the most successful and feared 'firm' in the capital.

The family 'business' is run by three brothers – Terry, the eldest, Patsy and Tommy. And their impressive history of acquittals at the Old Bailey has driven the Old Bill up the wall for years. All now well into their 40s, the A-Team come from a family of eleven brought up on the notorious Barnsbury Council Estate, on the less posh side of Islington, where their parents George and Florence still live to this day. It's just a stone's throw from Prime Minister Tony Blair's old home.

The A-Team kicked off their criminal careers when the brothers were at school and started leaning on other kids for their pocket money. Then they graduated to small-time street thieving before moving on to lucrative local protection rackets, intimidating stall-holders in street markets.

But the Adamses never forgot their roots and remained in the area renowned in the Sixties and early Seventies for local gangs such as the Nash Brothers. By the mid-Seventies the A-Team had started taking part in some tasty blaggings. They were already three steps up the ladder and no one had the bottle to get in their way.

In those early days, Patsy Adams was linked to a string of blaggings using high-powered motorbikes as getaway vehicles. The proceeds of these crimes were invested in a variety of convenient local cash businesses such as minicab firms and car washes. Then the brothers decided to buy themselves into the drinking clubs business – legal and illegal. One tavern – the Ra-Ra in Islington's Upper Street – soon became a favourite haunt for football stars from the local team, Arsenal.

The A-Team then spread themselves as far south as Hatton Garden's jewellery district. In 1983, Tommy Adams joined forces with a number of south London faces to play a role in the Brink's-Mat robbery at Heathrow. His alleged share of the £25 million pounds' worth of gold did more than anything to help the Adams boys reaffirm their power and influence north of the Thames.

Then Patsy Adams began steering the A-team towards the drugs explosion of the Eighties. Using some of those millions from the Brink's-Mat blagging, they began 'investing' in huge shipments of puff and Charlie. In 1984, Patsy was nicked for handling drugs but later acquitted.

Throughout this period the A-Team were collecting friendly, greedy Old Bill like kids collect Dinky toys. As their powerbase grew, the brothers realised they could use drugs as currency to bring pressure and influence on judges and politicians. Meanwhile, their ownership of clubs had spread into the lucrative West End and even as far west as Fulham on the other side of London from their home manor.

One club owner in West London told me a few years back, 'The Adamses sent a couple of their chaps down to see me because they knew I was up to my eyes in debt and they wanted to buy the club for a knockdown price. I didn't argue with them. They chucked me a few grand and I was out the door in munutes. I didn't want any aggro.'

Legitimate owners of some of the most 'respectable' clubs in Central London found themselves being pressurised by the A-Team, who wanted their teams of drug dealers to be given exclusive access to certain wealthy establishments. One of their favourite targets was a bunch of pubs and clubs in West London's trendy King's Road, where high-spending stockbrokers had developed a real nose for cocaine.

The A-Team didn't hesitate to lean on people who got in

their way. High-profile associates were plied with free sex and drugs and then 'milked' for help. The Adams team weren't shy about sticking shooters in people's faces, either.

One time Patsy was involved in a legendary incident while out at his villa near Marbella, on the Costa del Sol. Rumour has it that he cut the ear off the son of another famous British gangster during a fight in a restaurant over some missing drug money. On another occasion back in London, police raided Patsy's house in the North London suburbs and found a gun and a complete set of bullet-proof body armour. He wriggled out of that one by claiming it all belonged to his wife.

One of the A-Team's most notorious and feared enforcers was West Indian Gilbert Wynter – who later disappeared amid rumours that he'd been murdered after trying to double-cross the Adamses. Back in 1992, Wynter and Terry Adams, both armed, were nicked by the Old Bill as they were on their way to settle a dispute over a drugs deal. The A-Team's reputation had always been built on their willingness to take care of business personally when it really mattered.

Gilbert Wynter had for many years provided the brothers with invaluable links to black drug dealers and Yardies in North London. In 1994 he was nicked for the murder of former British athletics champion Claude Mosley. Mosley was executed after being called to a house in Stoke Newington to discuss claims that he was short-changing his suppliers – the A-Team. After

Mosley produced a gun, Gilbert Wynter virtually sliced him in half with a Samurai sword.

Wynter later walked free from the Old Bailey when the main witness refused to give evidence and was sent to prison for contempt of court. The judge at the time condemned the fact that 'a man who can commit this kind of crime can get away with it'.

In order to 'lose' the vast profits from their many criminal activities, the A-Team decided in the early Nineties to try to invest their money more wisely. Terry Adams and Gilbert Wynter were even spotted regularly attending business meetings at the plush Harley Street offices of a top corporate lawyer. In fact, he was a former bankrupt who rated himself a financial wizard capable of arranging large loans for the right deals.

One geezer who came across the bankrupt at the time described him as 'looking like an out-of-work gangster'. Unfortunately, he managed to lose a small fortune of the A-Team's hard-earned funds. Not long afterwards he was kidnapped and held at an hotel in Glasgow by some local Adams family associates. The A-team summoned him to London for discussions and gave him a right pasting in the process. He took the next one-way flight to Spain and didn't return for five years.

Around this time the A-Team added loan sharking to their long list of 'businesses' – lending money at punitive rates to any mug who'd been given the big heave-ho by the regular high street banks. One businessman with criminal connections was put under so much pressure to repay a debt to the Adamses that he sought out the help of a former Kray associate 'to settle the dispute'. That contact went and had a word with the Adamses but returned a couple of hours later with the stark message: 'You'd better bloody pay up or they'll 'ave you.' When another old school villain, Richardsons enforcer 'Mad' Frankie Fraser, tried to muscle in on an A-Team-controlled rave club in Clerkenwell he did a runner and hasn't been seen on the Adamses' manor since.

Property and drug dealer Michael Olymbious was not so lucky. He was bankrupt and borrowed a ton of cash from the Adamses. Then all his business deals went belly up and he fled to Cyprus to avoid his bankers. But, as they say in the underworld, you can run but you can't hide.

In 1996 Olymbious slipped back into London to see his family. Then he agreed to attend a meeting in south London the night before he was due to fly back to Cyprus. As he got out of his car a lone shootist fired a single bullet which went right through his head.

One of Olymbious's failed property deals involved the Beluga nightclub, in Finchley Road, North London. The Adamses turned it into the epicentre of their criminal empire. By 1994 the club was sponsoring world-title fights featuring Chris Eubank and promoted by Barry Hearn, at that time Britain's top promoter – though neither had any idea of the club's links with the Adams family, or any reason to think it wasn't a perfectly respectable venue. As soon as Hearn got to know about their connections, when a tabloid exposed the club's links with the Adams family, he severed his sponsorship links.

The A-Team, like the Krays before them, have carefully nurtured contacts in high places. Back in 1996, one Tory MP came under close scrutiny from detectives and MI5 officers trying to break the family's stranglehold on London's clubland. The politician even owned a private company which supplied the boys with an arsenal of weapons, including sub-machine guns, from former Eastern bloc countries.

That same MP is a highly-rated member of the A-Team's inner circle. But, unlike their predecessors the Krays, the Adamses don't want a high-profile lifestyle which would focus attention on their activities. They've always steered clear of most of their club interests 'Up West' and stuck to a small number of trusted old north London haunts. Within their close circle of associates, however, are several top-flight football stars, boxers and other minor celebrities.

In the summer of 1997, the A-Team had the front to put it around that they'd donated thousands of pounds to the Labour Party just before their historic 1997 landslide victory over the Tories. Tommy Adams told associates he made several payments to the party through two henchmen, Michael Papamichael and Edward Wilkinson, both later jailed for other Adams-related offences. But since gifts of less than £5,000 do not have to be publicly disclosed by political parties, it seems unlikely we'll ever hear the real story behind these allegations.

The A-Team also invested a lot of their dirty money in the world of horse racing through a successful businessman, long since fingered by the Old Bill as one of the Adamses' closest associates. He has been linked to race-fixing at meetings across the country. Organised crime investigators had kept an eye on him for years. In 1998, detectives raided his luxury apartment in West London, which just happens to be near to some of the A-Team's most profitable clubs. Unfortunately for the Old Bill, the man in question was at his villa in a Spanish village, near Marbella, close to the Costa Del Sol's biggest horse racing track.

This man's links to the Adamses go back several years. On one occasion, two armed high-ranking Adams enforcers were arrested on their way to resolve a dispute with which he was involved. Through him, the A-Team is reckoned to have forged close connections to specific jockeys and bookmakers involved in race-fixing. The Adams brothers have made huge profits from betting on horse racing. They've even purchased properties in London and the home counties with six-figure cheques from well-known bookmakers.

The police are unhappy to this day about Tommy Adams's acquittal of involvement in the £25 million Brink's-Mat gold bullion blagging in 1983. Later, Patsy pulled off a similar miracle escape after being nicked for importing 3.5 tons of cannabis, worth an estimated £25 million. He was acquitted, although his partner ended up copping 11 years when the case finally came to trial in 1993.

Certainly, at times the A-Team's power and influence seems to know no boundaries. In 1998, an official with the Crown Prosecution Service took a bribe from the brothers and leaked confidential information about their activities when the police were breathing down their necks. At the time, Tommy Adams was facing prosecution for drug trafficking and his brothers were interested in any information they could get their hands on. CPS snout Mark Herbert knew exactly who the Adams family were because his old man was a copper!

Herbert, a £14,000-a-year administration officer working at the CPS headquarters in London, took the names of informants off a CPS computer file. As Victor Temple, QC, later told a court, 'It needs little imagination of what might happen if the name of police informants fell into the wrong hands.' Fortunately detectives intercepted the names, which had been handwritten.

In fact, that case in September 1998 involving Tommy Adams ended up being Plod's only real result in their ongoing war with the A-Team. Tommy got a seven-and-a-half-year stretch for puff importation. In public, the police were delighted to have finally made charges stick on an A-Team member but Tommy – chewing gum and laughing as he was taken down to begin his sentence – saw it in a different light.

The Old Bill had confiscated £1 million cash of estimated drug profits from Adams, but they'd hoped for at least £6 million.

But what got most of London's big firms talking was the rumour that the rest of the A-team had 'allowed' the prosecution to go through to teach wildman Tommy a lesson because he'd been setting up drug deals behind the back of the rest of the family. 'The brothers went to see Tommy in Belmarsh Prison,' one Adams associate later explained. 'They told him they were dumping him because he'd gone behind their backs. He'd been caught freelancing and he was paying for it. They could have gone and bribed the jury – £1 million is not a problem – or given him the bullet, so he got off pretty lightly.'

The nicking of Tommy Adams had followed years of painstaking surveillance and detective work by an elite team from the National Crime Squad which had targeted the A-Team from a secret headquarters in Hertfordshire. They found that, officially, the family never existed. Police couldn't trace any bank accounts or records that showed whether Tommy and the others had ever been employed or paid tax.

In May 1999, the A-Team's 'influence' in criminal courts returned with a vengeance when Plod went for a prosecution over a torturing case. David McKenzie was a wealthy 46-year-old financier with an office in Mayfair, in the centre of London's West End. McKenzie laundered drug money for the Adams family, but those investments took a nose-dive and he lost close to £2 million of the A-Team's dirty dosh.

Terry Adams's golf partner Chris McCormack, 44 – a close associate of all three brothers – stood trial at the Old Bailey accused of causing McKenzie grevious bodily harm with intent. McKenzie said he'd been summoned to a meeting at Terry Adams's mansion in the North London suburb of Finchley for 'a discussion'.

By this time Terry was privately acknowledged as 'the chief exec of the Adams family board'. He'd become the boss and brains behind the A-Team over the previous ten years. McKenzie's courtroom testimony confirmed Terry's status as the main man. 'Everyone stood up when he walked in,' McKenzie explained. 'He looked like a star … a cross between Liberace and Peter Stringfellow. He was immaculately dressed, in a long black coat and white frilly shirt. He was totally in command.'

Big Terry Adams wanted all the family's cash returned by McKenzie, so when the financier failed to deliver, things got nasty. McKenzie later said that during a showdown at another gangster's house in Islington, North London, Terry Adams's golf partner McCormack – all 6ft 1in and 15 stone of him – kicked and beat McKenzie to a pulp in a vicious attack. McKenzie was slashed with a Stanley knife, which, according to one detective, left him with more lines than a map of the London Underground. Two of his tendons were permanently severed in the attack, affecting his ability to move his hands. His nose and left ear were left 'flapping off' by slivers of skin. And three ribs were broken.

When McKenzie finally took the stand at the Old Bailey trial, the gasps of shock were audible. 'He was in a right mess,' said one observer. 'They'd cut him to ribbons.'

First in the dock was Terry Adams's brother-in-law, John Potter, at whose house the attack took place. He claimed that McKenzie had been attacked in the house by a complete stranger! Detectives weren't impressed with his story. When it came to Big Chris McCormack's turn in the dock, he coughed to meeting David McKenzie three times because he was trying to recover the debt, 'as a favour to my old mate Patsy'. DNA samples of McKenzie's blood were found splattered on McCormack's motorbike jacket but heavyweight McCormack suggested they'd come from an earlier meeting when he'd broken up a fight between McKenzie and another man.

The Old Bailey jury of six men and six women deliberated for a day and were then sent to a hotel for the night – with round-the-clock armed police protection. At lunchtime the next day both enforcers were acquitted. As Big Chris McCormack heard the verdict, he said, 'Thank you,' to the jury and then added, 'Come and have a drink with me over the pub.'

Big Chris McCormack is regarded as Terry Adams's right-hand man. He would have been a real scalp for the police, but they weren't surprised he walked. These sort of acquittals involving the Adams family continue to be par for the course.

However, the A-Team knew they were pushing their luck after that narrow escape, so over the last couple of years they've been winding down some of their operations. Patsy spends most of his time in Spain and has his fingers in a lot of pies on the Costa Del Sol. Tommy's out of nick and living with his family in a £750,000 Georgian house in Mylne Street, King's Cross, while Terry continues living in an unassuming suburban house in North London, which naturally bristles with CCTV, radar beam alarms and six-inch-thick bullet-proof windows.

The Adams family have reached a stage where the legends about them have become ever more fantastic. Rightly or wrongly, on a scale of one to ten the A-Team are still rated as 'ten times more scary than the Krays'. Underworld informants have linked them to at least 30 killings and they are still talked about in legendary terms as the inventors of the 'two-on-a-bike' hit.

One North London detective, who spent eight years working for the CID on the A-Team's manor, says that whenever there's a serious crime in the area the Adams name still comes up. 'It's got to the stage where, just like the Krays, they're being credited with things they haven't even done. The fact they've tried to keep things low key doesn't mean they're not still running the manor, even if one of them does spend most of his time abroad.'

The A-Team's rumoured decision to go into 'semi-retirement' is seen by many in the London underworld as evidence that they sensed time was running out for them. They've deposited most of their money abroad and many of their London clubs and other enterprises have recently been sold on to other gangsters. 'They're winding down their businesses,' one old face told me recently. 'They know the net's been closing on them and they've pushed their luck.'

Rumour has it that some of their most deadly rivals have started singing about the Adams's activities to the cops in order to force them out of London. 'They're not around to lean on people as before,' explains the old face. 'Some faces are comin' out of the woodwork and tryin' to stitch 'em up. Same thing happened years back with the Krays and the Richardsons. The A-Team was goin' right over the top at one stage and somethin' had to be done about them.'

On Friday, March 9, 2007, that prediction came true when Terry Adams was finally nailed after a controversial trial at the Old Bailey. The headline in a newspaper the day after his sentencing said it all: ADAMS FAMILY CRIME BOSS JAILED FOR 7 YEARS.

Sentencing Terry at the Old Bailey, Judge Timothy Pontius said he would have to serve at least half of his term in prison. Terry showed no emotion as he was ordered to pay back £750,000 worth of assets in a confiscation order. He had faced a maximum term of 14 years in jail. Terry had agreed to a plea bargain on the eve of what was likely to have been a costly four-month trial just weeks before his case was heard. In return, his sick wife Ruth, 46, was spared prosecution.

Prosecutors told the court Terry had amassed tens of millions of pounds from drugs and extortion and he got that seven-year sentence after agreeing to admit to money laundering. Terry, now 52, was dubbed 'head of London's Adams crime family' after pleading guilty to a £1.1 million money laundering scam, which prosecutors described as covering only a tiny proportion of his illicit fortune.

Yet despite admitting laundering money that had been obtained through crime, he was not convicted of the crimes themselves. The court heard that Terry was finally trapped by an MI5 probe, which uncovered the money laundering operation that spanned decades. During that period of time, the court heard how Terry had acquired a string of luxury homes across London, all of them stuffed with stolen antiques. 'It was a prosperous life and included flying around the world, staying in the most exclusive hotels and indulging a passion for expensive watches, jewellery, motorbikes and private education,' prosecutor Andrew Mitchell told the Old Bailey.

The court heard that when Terry was arrested police seized £500,000 worth of arts and antiques, £48,000 worth of jewellery and £59,000 of banknotes stuffed in a shoebox in his attic. 'He comes from a pedigree, as one of a family whose name had currency all of its own in the underworld,' added Mitchell.

Joanna Barnes, described as one of Terry's accomplices, was said to have helped Terry evade justice. She avoided jail but was ordered to pay a £5,000 fine and court costs of £2,500. A masked man on a motorcycle had shot her husband, Solly Nahmome, dead in 1998.

After the trial, legal sources said the investigation cost in the region of £50 million. Amazingly, Terry had even managed to secure legal aid. With remission Terry may get out of prison as early as 2010. He is also believed to be planning to appeal against his sentence.

After Terry's trial more details about his downfall came to light. It emerged that MI5, looking for work after the Cold War ended, had turned its sights on Terry. Scotland Yard and MI5 then set up a secret squad to dismantle the Adams organisation. Codenamed Operation Trinity, they placed electronic bugs in the lounge, bedroom and loft of Terry's north London home.

Then the Inland Revenue started asking Terry to explain how he had got his £2 million house. Terry invented a range of occupations, including jeweller and public relations executive. Transcripts of the surveillance proved he was lying.

On 18 May 2007 Terry was ordered to pay £4.7 million in legal fees to three law firms who'd initially represented him under the UK's free legal aid scheme. He was also required to pay £0.8 million in prosecution costs. A few days later, on 21 May 2007, he was also ordered to file reports setting out his income for the next ten years.

However, as another retired gangster said recently, 'Don't think is the last you'll ever hear about the A-Team. Blokes like them never retire …'

CHAPTER
2

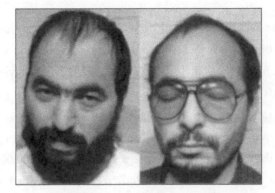

THE ARIFS

'Sometimes it'd be nice to wipe out the past. But you can't do that, can you? People never let you forget. That's just the way it is. You have to take life on the chin.'

DOGAN ARIF

A2, DARTFORD, KENT, MARCH 1976

The Securicor van had been shadowed all over south east London as it picked up takings from more than a dozen shops. Just as the vehicle drove up the busy A2 dual carriageway towards its depot in Powdermill Lane, Dartford, a gang of blaggers in two stolen motors forced it off the road.

Brandishing sawn-offs, the team ordered the Securicor guards out of the van and helped themselves to more than £100,000 – big money in those days. The windscreen was smashed with a sledgehammer, but when the robbers started spraying bullets around one of the guards was hit and later died. As passing motorists looked on in amazement, the gang escaped by running up an embankment. A number of motorists even photographed them. The police soon rounded up all the usual suspects. This is the hard-nosed blagging that put the Arif family on the map.

Ozer Arif, then 28 and a mini-cab proprietor of Layard Square, Southwark, was later charged with murder along with two other men. Bekir Arif, then 22 and described as a butcher, of Hawkestone Road, Rotherhithe, had his murder charges withdrawn, but he was also nicked for robbery, stealing cars, possessing guns without certificates and disposing of them.

In May 1977, Ozer Arif pleaded not guilty to the murder charges at the Old Bailey. At the end of a four-week trial the jury also found him not guilty of wounding two other guards with intent to cause them grevious bodily harm, and possessing shotguns with intent to commit robbery. Meanwhile, brother Bekir got a five-stretch after coughing to robbery.

Afterwards, the Old Bill proudly announced they had broken the back of the Arifs. They boasted to reporters, 'This is the best news we have had for a long time. We reckon we've nipped them in the bud.'

They couldn't have been more wrong.

After Ozer Arif's acquittal, he threw a 'celebration' party he even sent an invitation to the widow of the guard shot dead during the blagging. As they say in the underworld, he felt he should make a gesture.

The Arif family and their army of associates have gone on to make millions thanks to a series of blaggings, highly lucrative drug-trafficking operations and a whole bunch of legitimate businesses set up with stolen cash.

One retired thief taker, who's spent half a lifetime digging into the Arif family background, told me a few years back that the brothers' father was given a new identity by the British Army in Cyprus when he became an informant for the British back in the Fifties. 'He was given a safe house over here and a new identity. That's how the Arif family came to live in south east London. Bloody ironic, isn't it? We helped set up the Arifs as one of the most awesome gangs of villains ever seen in London.'

* * *

The Arifs first emerged as a force to be reckoned with in the Seventies when the family ran a cafe off Deptford Broadway, right in the heart of their adopted homeland of south east London. Oldest brother, Dogan, soon earned himself a reputation as a geezer with a chirpy sense of humour and a fondness for sticking shooters in people's mouths when he wanted to make an important point.

One of the first times Dogan did this was in a pub in Rotherhithe in 1979. Witnesses swear to this day that he pointed his sawn-off right in his victim's face before panning the weapon at this fellow's shoulder and squeezing the trigger. No one in that boozer remembered seeing a thing when the Old Bill later arrived on the scene.

Frightened witnesses always get so confused, and the Arifs had just created a pub full of frightened witnesses. If the Old Bill had tried to get a photofit from the descriptions provided by those punters, they'd have ended up searching for The Elephant Man.

It was a similar tale when Dogan's kid brother Dennis walked into another tavern in South London and fronted up a geezer who owed him some readies. Dennis pushed his Uzi into this bloke's face before playing a sick and twisted game of pizzicato on the poor bastard's belly with a flick knife. Like all major players, the Arifs use fear as their number one weapon. A lot of folk see them strutting round their manor like medieval warlords, building a reputation as bandits who specialise in violent crimes with maximum profits.

During those early days, the Arifs also built up vast reserves of cash from legitimate businesses such as jewellery and menswear stores, a restaurant and a nightclub. Many wondered why the hell they needed the fix of robbery and drugs when everything straight was coming up roses. Their club – The Connoisseur – was a legendary gaff done out in black and shiny chrome on the Old Kent Road. Every face for miles around wanted to be seen on the premises.

Then Dogan and Dennis ran into a heavy bunch of coke dealers inside The Connoisseur. The Arif boys took it upon themselves to 'confiscate' the merchandise. Turned out these fellows had been transporting the drugs for the Mafia who were not happy when they heard what had happened. Dogan and Dennis barricaded themselves inside the club with submachine guns and spent two tense weeks in a stand-off refusing to budge until all parties had reached a satisfactory agreement.

Dogan has even used some of the Arif money to support and manage his own football team, Fisher Athletic. Under his guidance the Docklands club achieved remarkable success a few years back. They were promoted out of the local league into the GM Vauxhall Conference and, as sponsorship money poured in, they got within a whisper of the old Fourth Division.

In 1988, the police tried to come down on the Arifs like the proverbial ton of truncheons. The cops even set up a special squad reinforced by men from the customs investigation branch with the express purpose of getting the Arifs. Chop them off at the kneecaps before they take over south east London. Tens of thousands of quid was chucked around in a bid to grease their rivals' palms.

Then Dogan went and got himself nicked riding shotgun on a lorry that was supposed to contain £8 million quid's worth of puff, although Customs officers had already removed the stash and replaced it with chipboard. Dogan swears blind to this day that he was fitted up for that job. He copped a nine-stretch. His mates still say to this day that he was never on the lorry tracked by the cops and Customs officers. He later appealed against his sentence and it was reduced to three years.

In many of the pubs and bodybuilding gyms of south east London, it's said the Arifs have always been clever at stashing away their millions before the long arm of the law can lay its hands on the money. And the Arifs might have kept a cleaner sheet if Dogan and his brothers hadn't made the fatal error of getting directly involved in their own action.

As one retired blagger explained, 'The geezers who stay out of the nick are the ones who never dirty their own hands. They're the fellows who finance the teams who do the actual blaggings or the drug deals. The Arifs should have taken a step back and avoided direct involvement.'

But behind the scenes Dogan and his boys wanted complete and utter respect so they found themselves obliged to get involved in a few tasty gangland battles as a matter of honour. 'They felt they had no choice but to come out fighting,' says one former Arif associate. 'They wanted other faces on the manor to know they don't take no shit off no one.'

In November 1990, the Arifs hit the headlines once again when brothers Dennis and Mehmet plus brother-in-law Anthony Downer tried to pull off the blagging of a Securicor van in Woodhatch, near Reigate, in Surrey. But the Sweeney got a tip off and armed police lay in wait when the Arif family members and another sidekick struck. They were all nicked on the spot except for blagger Kenny Baker who was shot dead by the police after he and Mehmet decided not to throw down their weapons. The gang was carrying a Brazilian-made revolver, a 12-bore Browning shotgun, a US Army self-loading Colt, an Enfield Mark II revolver and a Browning 1922 pistol. Later that same day, the Old Bill doorstepped a house in Streatham, South London, where they seized a small arsenal of weapons, including three sawn-offs and a sub-machine gun. Mehmet eventually put his hands up to the attempted blagging but Dennis refused to cough and was later found guilty in court.

What really shocked other south east London faces at the time was that Dennis and Mehmet had even bothered to dirty their hands by going across the pavement when they already enjoyed millionaires' lifestyles on their home turf of south east London. 'It's always baffled us. Why the hell didn't they stay away from the action?' says one old Catford face.

NEW KRAYS SMASHED read the massive front page headline in the *Sun* back in December '91 when those two members of the Arif family were finally sent down after trying to rob that security van carrying £1 million. The police proudly screened video footage of the arrest and tried to suggest that the Arifs were now a spent force. But others knew they were far from dead and buried.

Shortly after the brothers were sent down a heavyweight contest was declared between a brace of south east London firms, many of whom suspected the other had grassed up the Arifs and their gang of blaggers. Round one kicked off in March 1991, when the Arifs' cousin Abby Abdullah walked into William Hill's bookies, in Bagshott Street, Walworth, with his bull-terrier on the end of a lead.

Minutes later, a hitman squeezed off two rounds from his 9mm Browning after Abby was fingered by a helpful punter. Abby had even tried to use another customer in the betting shop as a shield but was shot again in the back as he ran from the premises. He then managed to stagger 400 yards to a friend's house on the Kingslake Estate, where he keeled over at the front door. That's when Abby whispered the names of his alleged killers. Soon half the manor heard he'd named a couple of gangsters.

Unemployed mechanic Ginger Horton, 51, told what happened after he found Abby bleeding on his doorstep. 'Abby gasped, "I've been shot. I've been shot … I'm going. I'm going." ' Horton went on, 'He tried to sit on a chair. But he fell off on to the floor with blood gushing out of his back. I pulled his shirt up and saw two small bullet holes – one at the top and one at the bottom of his back. These cowards have murdered one of the nicest blokes you could ever wish to meet. He only got out of prison a couple of years ago after being put away as a teenager. He was on life parole. I don't know what he went in for but I can't believe it's got anything to do with this – it happened so long ago.'

Abby was rushed by air ambulance to the Royal Hospital, Whitechapel, where he was pronounced dead shortly after arrival. When the news of Abby's death was broken by the Arif brothers to their old man, Yusef, who had treated Abby as a son, he went ballistic and the word revenge was on everyone's lips.

In June 1991, a London face was nicked for the Abby shooting by some out-of-town coppers brought in from a special crime unit. They later claimed he told them, 'I didn't mean him to die. I didn't mean it.'

Then one night a well-known face was shot in the Arif's club, The Connoisseur. This fellow, who survived, naturally refused to say who shot him. Three days later in King's College Hospital he spewed up the bullet that grounded him only to then promptly swallow it again. 'He wanted to stop us doing forensic tests on it,' one plain clothes cop later helpfully explained. 'And you gotta remember these people like to settle things their own way.'

That shooting undoubtedly contributed towards the gunning down of a well-known villain the middle of 1991. As he was shot, one of the killers screamed, 'This one's for Abby.'

The plugging of this villain was performed by two fellows wearing ski masks. They've never been fingered, but a lot of people reckon one of them was the legendary Jimmy 'Big Jim' Moody, an East End armed robber who escaped from Brixton nick with IRA man Gerard Tuite in 1980. While on the run, Moody legged it across the Irish Sea and made a living as a freelance hitman who iced at least half a dozen geezers, including some well-known Protestant paramilitaries.

In June 1993, Big Jim Moody paid the ultimate price by being gunned down at The Royal pub in Hackney by a lone gunman.

Down at Parkhurst on the Isle of Wight, Dennis and Mehmet Arif were serving 18 and 22 years for that armed blagging.

One screw explained, 'We are not dealing with a bunch of naughty schoolboys. The regime cannot cope.' And another screw who clashed with the Arif brothers moaned, 'It's a situation beyond control because they [the Arifs] run the wing. Searches of visitors' toilets often unearth stashes of cannabis, crack and cocaine.'

Another screw later told me, 'What d'you expect? Drugs help keep inmates more peaceful a lot of the time. No one wants them pacing their cells getting tense and nasty. It's better if they're chilled out in a daze on their bunks, ain't it?'

Dennis and Mehmet, jailed for that £750,000 security van raid at Woodhatch, Surrey, were even rumoured to have mobiles and a couple of shooters in their cells. Some Parkhurst staff were so spooked they asked for outside protection from the brothers.

The screws feared attacks on their families after clashing with the Arifs on D-wing.

One screw explained, 'A prisoner in D-wing head-butted a senior warder so hard his retina was detached. The inmate was segregated, but was back in 24 hours because of the Arifs. We were all disgusted.'

Another time, a warden was injured after skidding on two packets of cocaine lying in a corridor (I kid thee not). He was last heard of threatening to sue the prison authority. And those screws who still patrolled the Arifs' wing found they could no longer use the specially installed security viewers to take a look inside cells.

'All the spyholes are blocked by curtains, paint or paper,' groaned one fed-up officer. Dennis and Mehmet are due back out in the real world some time next year.

In October 1997, two more of the Arif boys, Bekir and Michael, were pulled by detectives investigating a plot to flood the streets with more than £10 million worth of heroin. The police claimed they found 95 kilos of the drug piled up in the front room of a South London house raided by them.

The Old Bill's swoop marked the end of a lengthy undercover operation by Scotland Yard's elite Organised Crime Group which was set up to combat Mafia-style villains like the Arifs. Detectives reckoned Bekir and Michael were running a major drug-trafficking and distribution network. Car dealer Bekir, 44, was charged with conspiracy to supply heroin while Michael Arif was released pending further enquiries.

In May 1999, Bekir, at the time 46 and living in a £250,000 house in Petts Wood, Kent, was jailed for 23 years after being convicted of conspiracy to supply heroin. The court was told that Bekir had used his second-hand car business as a front to supply £12 million worth of heroin.

The court also heard that the cops had spent a year watching his car business in Rotherhithe and a nearby flat. The jury were even played tapes of conversations recorded by sophisticated listening devices and shown photos of the main players in action.

In court Bekir, known by now as 'The Duke', insisted he was nothing more than a 'Del Boy' businessman. It didn't help when prosecutors pointed out Bekir was splashing out 30 grand a year for an executive box to watch the Arsenal. Judge Geoffrey Grigson told Bekir, 'Your role was plainly that of principal and your conduct was as cynical and dishonest as has been your defence. In my view there is no mitigation.'

I recently met up with Dogan Arif at his business address, a fruit and ciggie machine service centre in a dead-end street, just off the Old Kent Road. 'I'll see you on the cameras and come and get you,' he told me on the phone an hour before our meet. As I drove my old jalopy slowly towards a brick wall that marked the end of the road, I wondered what he really meant. The idea of Dogan Arif coming to get me sent a shiver up my spine.

In the not too distant past, Dogan's favourite way of getting anyone's attention had been to stick a shooter in their face and ask questions later. As one-time unofficial godfather of the Arif family, his reputation precedes him with everyone from the major faces in London to the police at Scotland Yard. Dogan is respected by them all – a true guv'nor of guv'nors.

The CCTV cameras that pan the end of the lane where he has his one-armed bandit warehouse command a view of rundown buildings and lots of broken glass shattered across the pavement. It's just a stone's throw from their old club, The Connoisseur. As I slung my old Merc up on the kerb, a Doberman the size of a small donkey came bounding out of a side-door.

Just then a tall, dark-haired, bull-necked bouncer-type yanked the pooch back into the front office of the warehouse. Inside, a pretty girl in her early twenties offered me a cuppa and told me that Dogan would be out 'any minute'. It was all very civilised.

Then the man himself emerged grinning and full of charm. He walked me through the small warehouse, filled with flashing machines, into his office. Compact, muscular and moving with an athlete's roll, I was instantly reminded that he was once a talented footballer. Many reckon Dogan could have made it as a pro, but he had bigger fish to fry.

It turned out Dogan was still miffed about how he'd been nicked for that £8 million puff deal back in 1988. His brief reckoned if he'd been anyone else the conviction would have been completely thrown out. Dogan shrugs his shoulders when he tells you this. That's the way it goes, ain't it?

Back then, Dogan claims, the police confiscated everything, including half the family mansion in Catford. They even closed down his pride and joy – The Connoisseur club. As Dogan later told me, 'I didn't have a penny when I got out in July 1993. For six months I did nothing. I was lost. Three years is a lot of time to sort your head out, set out your stall in life.'

Dogan told me he'd turned over a new leaf. Gone straight. But it's not easy teaching an old dog new tricks. Behind the charming smile, Dogan's old brain was churning over more money-making schemes than Al Pacino in *Scarface*. One old thief taker I know still calls him to this day, 'the thinking man's gangster'. While Dogan was banged up in Parkhurst the governor even encouraged him to talk to prison visitors because he had such a sharp take on life inside. He's a smart fellow, knows how to spin a neat sentence together and he's got a superb take on life.

'Sometimes it'd be nice to wipe out the past,' Dogan told me. 'But you can't do that, can you? People never let you forget. That's just the way it is. You have to take life on the chin.'

When I met Dogan he said everything he was into was purely legit; leasing cigarette vending machines and assorted one-armed bandits to pubs and clubs throughout south east London. But it's difficult to imagine that his reputation doesn't impress the customers. 'I split the profits of each machine fifty/fifty with the owner of every place I supply.'

Of course, the Old Bill on the manor insist Dogan's only keeping a low profile because he knew he'd cop a 15-year stretch next time around. 'I couldn't handle that,' Dogan admitted to me. Only a few weeks before our meet, Dogan had popped down to Parkhurst to see his old mate Eddie Richardson while he was visiting brothers Mehmet and Dennis.

Dogan says to this day that drugs are rotting the very core of gangsterdom. He reckons about 80% of those faces heavily involved in drug deals are taking the same poison they're peddling. 'That makes a lot of them unstable. All the rules have been thrown out the window. You can't predict anythin'. These chaps are out of control. It's like an army no one can command. How can you control people who can't control themselves? There's no respect, no code any more. Years ago I might pick up the phone and say, "Look, that mustn't happen. Cut it out." Now, the chances are they'll say, "Who the hell are you? Piss off!" The game's changed. The chaps are no longer in control.'

Dogan reckons the big families of the Eighties and Nineties are on the way out. 'They had principles and respect. The police could keep things under control 'cause people were predictable.

Now there are hundreds of operators all over the place climbin' on the bandwagon. It's too easy by half. Let's say Billy Bloggs has a transport company. He'll move a consignment of drugs. Suddenly he's got more money than he's ever dreamed of. Now he's in the underworld. He's got to have soldiers. But he doesn't know what he's doing, he knows nothin' about it, but he's in it. It's chaos. There's no respect and no control. You can't blame the public if they want the police to throw the rules out of the window. And they do. They infiltrate, they pay big money to grasses. There's electronic surveillance, MI5. If you have things you care about – a family – don't even think about it any more.'

Dogan sounds well convincing. At the time I met him he was definitely trying to stay on the straight and narrow and he was trying to avoid the limelight. But that doesn't stop him being asked for his opinions in certain south east London taverns where he remains a respected hardman, a feared gangster who knows what's what.

'I get pestered by people who want to talk about the old days the minute I walk into certain places. It drives me mad. They call up the champagne, slap me on the back. I'd rather have a bottle of wine at home with my family.'

Dogan blames a lot of it fairly and squarely at the feet of the OTT 1980s. 'Everyone had money in the Eighties. Everyone was spending like crazy. There'd be kids with five grand in their pocket. They'd say, "Give us a gram of Charlie.

What the hell, make it five grams." They'd ask me for it. I'd sling them out, the idiots.'

Despite his family being linked to the supply of mountains of drugs, Dogan swears blind he's fiercely anti-narcotics. 'When I was a kid I was in the jungle. There is only one way out of the jungle – you fight your way out. But I've done it. That stuff is a killer, believe me.'

Dogan reckons his legit businesses, his family and Fisher Athletic FC are all that matter to him now. The club slipped back into obscurity during his stretch in the nick. But by the time I caught up with him, Dogan had returned as technical director and he was convinced he could help lead Fisher back to the glory days.

Then our conversation turned to one of the 1990s most notorious south east London gangsters whose name was top of all the Most Wanted Lists. 'He's bad news for all of us. He caused us a lot of heat and I hope he's six feet under 'cause we can do without his kind,' Dogan said. 'Where I come from you keep things low key. You don't draw attention to yourself in the way this fellow has. Sure, I've met him in the past but he's not someone I'd ever do business with.'

Dogan says that the gangster is motivated by greed and drugs. 'Fuckin' drugs have caused a lot of these problems. Now the stakes are so fuckin' high that knockin' off a chap is done without anyone even givin' a toss. It's tragic and we're all goin' to end up six feet under at this rate. We're all destroying ourselves.'

Meanwhile some of Dogan's brothers may be currently under lock and key but rest assured their fortune hasn't disappeared. As one recently retired cop told me recently, 'We'll be lucky if we get our hands on a tenth of their money. They've been clever at distributing it. And once they're out they'll no doubt be involved in all sorts of nonsense.'

Despite a few local difficulties, the Arif brothers – Ozer, Dennis, Mehmet and Dogan – are far from dead and buried having copped a multi-million-pound fortune thanks to the lucrative drugs trade that mushroomed in the late Eighties and early Nineties.

'Sure, there are other tasty characters on the manor these days, but these guys have still got a fearsome reputation,' says one old lag.

The Arifs are not to be crossed …

CHAPTER
3

COCKY

**'He's ultra-intelligent, as
sharp as they come.'**

BRIEF KEVIN DOOLEY.

Curtis 'Cocky' Warren, complete with Desperate Dan pecs and a head shaved as round and smooth as a billiard ball, virtually has the word 'Gangster' stamped across his forehead. In some ways he's so obvious no one can take his reputation seriously. But many villains have found out to their cost that Cocky Warren is a deadly character with blood as cold as ice.

Cocky's one smart cookie. Streetwise, low key and very bright – and he's only in it for the very big money. This is a character who deals in hundreds of thousands of pounds worth of drugs every week.

As his arch enemies, the police, now openly admit, 'He might be nothin' much to look at, the usual Scouse lad in a shell suit, but he's one helluv an operator. He doesn't drink, smoke or use drugs. He's got a photographic memory for telephone numbers, bank accounts and the like. We've been looking for where he keeps his stuff. On a computer? In notes? No way. He carries it all inside his head.'

His nickname comes from 'Cocky Watchman' which is Scouse slang for a dodgy character. And in Liverpool he's been known for years as the Colombian Cali cartel's *primera* agent in northern Europe. This gangster is pure and utter evil and he's one of the richest villains in the land. He's even made it on to *The Sunday Times* Rich 500 list, the highest placed gangster ever to do so.

Cocky Warren makes the Krays look like amateurs. The Great Train Robbery and Brink's-Mat geezers, swaggering highwaymen from the pre-drugs era, are nothing more than second division. Curtis Warren is Premier League.

The key to Cocky's success is that until he came on the scene most villains got their drug shipments via middlemen. That meant they dealt in relatively small quantities. One hundred kilos was a major seizure for Customs and Excise ten years ago. Then Curtis Warren came on the scene and those smalltime operators soon faded into the background.

Cocky rapidly got himself a direct line to the biggest drug cartels in all four corners of the universe. Charlie from the Colombians; puff from the growers and fields of Morocco and Senegal; Europe's finest quality amphetamines and E from the top labs, mainly in Holland; and heroin from the poppy fields of Afghanistan.

And once Cocky had got the right financial backing he didn't even have to bother with cash upfront. Suppliers gave him virtually unlimited credit once he proved he could lay his hands on the cash. He'd get a shipment and then sell on a third of it to drug dealers in other European countries so that he was already in profit before his team hit the streets of Liverpool with the produce.

In his early days, the late Eighties, Cocky had been known for waving shooters in people's faces, but by the time the Nineties came around he was so powerful that he left all that to his team. No one crossed Cocky.

Smuggling coke, puff, smack and E is Cocky's full-time

profession and he's studied the best methods as closely as a scientist preparing a vaccine for cancer.

In Britain last year around £500 million worth of narcotics was seized by customs and police, but that's not even 5% of the gross national product. It's a trade worth tens of billions of pounds. Cocky Warren is the kingpin; a bulk buyer who knows exactly how to deal with the heaviest. 'Cocky's a man of honour. He never backs out once he's cut a deal and the Colombians reckon he is *numero uno*,' says one who should know.

The drug barons thrive because of one simple premise: supply and demand. More people snort a line, pop a pill or take a puff on a joint than ever before. A lot of them might call it stress relief, but all they're doing is lining the pockets of some of the most deadly faces this country has ever known.

The police keep trying to chip away at the gangsters but it's not easy. Cocky Warren and his crew have shelled out hundreds of thousands of quid in bribes to bent cops. And whenever the straight cops get close they seem to just fail at the final hurdle.

Cocky and his team reckon no amount of policing will ever wipe them out – and the vast profits continue to roll in. Even when multi-millionaire gangsters like Cocky are taken off the street and locked up their power and influence continues and their stashes of cash get bigger and bigger. Cocky has a long chain of command and no one dares cross him.

Cocky Warren's first brush with the law as a major dealer came in the late Eighties when one of his couriers was stopped at Dover with a Bible which had been hollowed out and packed with heroin. Persuaded to help the Old Bill, Warren's soldier went and called his boss at home and told him he 'had the drugs'. The phone line went dead before Cocky could incriminate himself. There was no case against him, but he was now a target for the cozzers. Cocky Warren, without a qualification to his name and apparently without a job, was heading for the sort of riches most of us can only dream about.

It was all a very different story when Curtis Francis Warren was born at home in Liverpool on 31 May 1963. His old man was a mixed-race sailor with the Norwegian Merchant Navy. His grandfather is even listed as a coffee manufacturer in the Americas. His mum, Sylvia Chantre, is the daughter of a shipyard boiler attendant.

Cocky was brought up in the Granby district of Toxteth, a bomb-damaged area of Liverpool wiped out by the Jerries during the last war and then re-flattened by the Toxteth riots in the early Eighties. When he was 12 he was nicked for joyriding. It's a hard manor where only the tough survive. Cocky quit school in his early teens and soon found himself in more trouble with the law for petty thieving. Then he honed his criminal skills snatching handbags and dealing in small amounts of puff.

He even hung around outside the gates of his old school selling wraps of heroin to local junkies. And he was picking up friends and acquaintainces as fast as a kerb crawler. One mate, Mike Ahearne, ended up on the TV show *Gladiators*. Another pal was Johnny 'Sonny' Phillips, a black bouncer who went on to became a fearsome enforcer – one of the toughest characters in Liverpool. Another mate was Stephen Mee, who later made a daring escape from a prison van in the middle of the Yorkshire moors.

The cops in Liverpool say Cocky soon moved up the criminal ladder by working on club doors as a bouncer. Then he began running a team of heavies organising security for various taverns. As one of his old mates explained, 'If you control the doors, you control the drugs.'

In 1988 came Cocky's biggest break. He hooked up with a notorious Liverpool businessman, known as 'The Banker' who'd made his first fortune hijacking lorries at Liverpool docks back in the Sixties. Half of Merseyside reckons The Banker had been backing drug operations on the manor for years. Renowned for his involvement in loads of crimes but without a nicking to this day. The Banker helped Warren make the leap from local supplier to regional trafficker by giving him the financial clout to steam in to the big drug boys. Cocky had serious ambitions to be the main wholesaler for the whole of north west England. Those who dealt with Cocky at the time knew he was a good operator. 'He's ultra-intelligent, as sharp as they come,' says his one-time brief, Kevin Dooley.

Within months, Cocky Warren became totally emersed in the coke trade, bigtime. Then he teamed up with another drug baron who worked the north east of England to Cocky's north west. These two characters pulled in so much dosh that they became multi-millionaires virtually overnight.

Jealous small-time gangsters across Liverpool started grassing up Cocky Warren's activities so he decided to nurture some important boys in blue. Merseyside senior detective Chief Inspector Elmore Davies, later jailed for five years for corruption for his part in trying to get one of Cocky's acquaintances off a firearms charge, was just one of Cocky's new best friends.

Then in September 1991, Cocky stepped on to the global drug stage when he and the drug baron travelled from Dover to Calais by ferry on British visitor passports. Accompanying them was Mario Halley, a 'marketing representative' for the Cali cartel in Colombia. Cocky and his two mates told immigration they were only travelling inside Europe. Then they drove to Brussels, where they parked their car before catching a plane to Malaga, Spain. From Malaga they went up to Madrid. Then Cocky and his accomplice took out their own ten-year regular passports and flew across to Caracas, Venzuela, which just happens to share its border with Colombia.

In South America, Warren was introduced to Camillo Jesus Ortiz, who headed up a company formed on behalf of the cartel – the Conar Corporation. Warren and his mate put down a £6 million deposit for two giant shipments of Charlie. The first, of 1.5 tonnes, would arrive in the port of Felixstowe the following month, October 1991. The coke would be hidden in steel boxes sealed inside lead ingots, which were not easy to slice open and impossible to X-ray.

Just before the shipment arrived, Cocky Warren flew to Amsterdam with two of his associates Anthony Cahill, 26, and Colin Smith to discuss the final details of the shipment. The team were re-introduced to Colombian Jesus Ortiz by the cartel's marketing man Mario Halley. Within days Warren and his team were given the nod that their goods were on the way and Mario Halley flew into Manchester where he was driven to Merseyside by Cocky to await the shipment.

Cocky and Halley arrived with special tools to remove 500kg of Charlie which Warren would then distribute in Britain, while the rest went to Holland and Greece. Cocky's distribution deal guaranteed he was already in profit before he'd even flogged a gram of his coke on Merseyside.

But before the shipment left Felixstowe, Dutch cops tipped off British customs that a major shipment of drugs was hidden in steel boxes inside the lead ingots. Customs even cut open one ingot in that first shipment from South America but found nothing.

The ingots were released and taken to a warehouse outside Liverpool. South American Halley was on site to extract the cocaine. The ingots were then buried in rubble at a mill before being sold for scrap, ending up in Newcastle.

A second shipment, of 900kg, left Venezuela in December that year. As it came in Cocky Warren and his accomplice were nicked. It looked as if the law had them bang to rights this time. But then certain cops, whose identities were never known, came forward and claimed the accomplice was an informer and should be given special treatment. They insisted he should be allowed to walk free so he could put the finger on some even bigger fish. The boys in blue eventually torpedoed the entire Customs' case. The accomplice was released and the case against Cocky Warren at Newcastle Crown Court collapsed in 1992.

Cocky was so chipper he spat at the Customs officers who'd pursued him: 'I'm off to spend my £87 million from the first shipment and you can't fuckin' touch me.' He boasted to associates that a number of his police contacts got handsomely rewarded for their unswerving loyalty after the case against him was thrown out.

Cocky's acquittal in Newcastle also sent a message to the cartels he dealt with across the globe. They now knew that, although Cocky had faced decades in the slammer, he'd kept his mouth shut. He'd never once offered to do a deal and turn grass. This was a man to be trusted. Being nicked was the best thing that ever happened to Cocky.

Certain straight-shooting cops, however, remained determined to nick him. Less than six months later, Customs officers conducted a covert search of a lorry at Felixstowe and found 250kg of heroin. They watched as it was driven to Burton Wood services on the M62; then, while it was parked, they saw Cocky drive into the compound. But then he spotted the surveillance officers and scarpered. 'He's got this built-in radar system – it's called his brain. He reckons he can sense any problems before they happen,' says one old associate.

Customs were naturally hopping mad. Both sides made important decisions that day. Customs launched Operation Crayfish to try and land the biggest fish of all – Curtis Warren. He was to get 24-hour round-the-clock surveillance with all the trimmings. And Cocky knew he'd need to have that radar switched on 24-hours-a-day.

Not long afterwards, £30,000 of Cocky's money was confiscated by the Old Bill during a raid on an associate's property. The small-time gangsters soon found the cash elsewhere and paid up Cocky within days. That's what villains call respect.

When the Moroccan Government tried to put the squeeze on the puff industry, Cocky flew over to North Africa and went out and bought people off; hotel staff, bankers and a bunch of coppers. 'That's what we call real class. He knew the key to his survival was greasing the right palms. It's what makes him such a big-time player,' says one in the know.

Cocky even tried to keep his motors low key. He was usually only seen out and about in a black Nexus, aircon as standard. He told one associate, 'It doesn't do you any good to be seen flashing it around. It winds people up.'

In the spring of 1995, Cocky's main man, Johnny Phillips, walked into a rundown Liverpool bar called Cheers and had a face-off with rival gangster, David Ungi, a former amateur boxing champ. Phillips, a steroid-pumping giant, was well pissed off at Ungi and told Cocky that Ungi deserved a good hiding 'or worse'.

On 1 May 1995, Ungi was shot dead at the wheel of his motor. It later emerged that a previous attempt to kill him had failed. A spate of shoot-outs followed the Ungi killing. Phillips himself was hit and seriously wounded in one attack. Although he survived, Phillips died the following year from heart failure after years of steroid and Charlie abuse.

Following the Ungi shooting, Liverpool descended into all-out gang war. That month – May 1995 – 11 people were shot. Yet virtually nobody was nicked. One fellow was sliced up so badly with a machete that it took seven hours for the coroner to join his body parts together in order to carry out a half-decent autopsy.

The wild-west-style antics of the drug-fuelled gangsters on the streets of his home town really got up Cocky Warren's nose. He quit Merseyside and set up home in Holland, although the police believe to this day that he was behind a lot of the shoot-outs himself. 'I think he realised that if he hung around someone was going to have a pop at him. Things were getting way too hot for him,' one detective says today.

Typically, Cocky Warren was soon running his drugs empire from Holland. Early in 1996 Customs intercepted 60 kilos of coke hidden inside a petrol tanker at Dover which they're convinced was *en route* to Cocky. Police also linked Cocky to a half ton of puff seized at another British port around the same time.

Cocky then decided to devise a more airtight system. He knew he had to stop taking any personal risks otherwise he'd end up under permanent lock and key. So shortly after arriving in Holland, Cocky set up a cellular network of drugs with each section working independently of the other. That meant if one part of the Warren organisation was busted then it wouldn't affect any of the other sections.

Cocky had settled in a modest Dutch town called Sassenheim in a villa called Bakara. He hung a boxer's punchbag from the attic ceiling and checked out the world from four slits in the roof. North, east, south and west were always covered. All alone in the big house with virtually no furniture, Warren spent hours every day gossiping to his old team back in Merseyside. What he didn't realise was that every call was being monitored by the Dutch police although he was smart enough never to refer to anyone by their real name – nicknames only.

They sounded like something out of an Elmore Leonard crime novel; The Vampire, Cracker, Macker and Tacker the Bell with no Stalk, the Egg on Legs, Lunty, Badger, Boo, Twit and Twat, Big Foot, the Big Fella, the J Fella, the L Fella and many more.

One time Warren gently stepped in between two brothers at the centre of a feud back in Liverpool. He talked to his family. It was clear Cocky missed Merseyside and, typically, despite already being a very rich man, he couldn't resist wheeling and dealing. He thrived on the excitement. In some ways, the buzz gave him more of a kick than the readies.

So while Curtis Warren was busy re-organising his empire, Operation Crayfish – 30 cops working full time to bring Cocky to justice – continued shadowing his every move. They wanted to pick off each of Cocky's commercial limbs, one by one. With the help of underworked spies at MI5 they stepped up surveillance to include phone taps and round-the-clock electronic intelligence gathering.

They believed one of the keys to nicking Cocky was to break up his swift and superbly organised money-laundering system, in which he cleverly manipulated currency exchange rates to cleanse tens of millions of pounds each year.

Meanwhile, Cocky Warren lived up to his reputation as a non-smoking teetotaller, who has probably still never tried any of the narcotics he's sold for such a vast profit. Despite being in Holland, he remained close to his girlfriend, Stephanie Glennan, the mother of his child. He even owned a private jet, as well as learning to fly helicopters, and indulged himself in loads of chunky gold jewellery.

And Cocky Warren showed immense generosity to those who did what he wanted. From Holland he paid out £50,000 each to two witnesses in a shooting trial of a close associate. Cocky even arranged for a Liverpool bodyguard to give £10,000 to his favourite detective via his old school pal and one-time *Gladiators* TV star Mike Ahearne.

Dutch police monitoring Cocky's phones tipped off Merseyside police and they dropped a camera into Warren's friend's flat, gathering enough evidence to bring about a successful prosecution of that bent copper. Ahearne was eventually jailed for being the go-between for Cocky and the corrupt cop.

A few months after setting up shop in Holland, Cocky sent one of his dodgier pals, Stephen Mee, already on the run from a 22-year sentence following an earlier escape from a prison van on the Pennines, to Colombia to arrange a 400kg shipment of Charlie. It was to be packed inside metal ingots just like the ones all those years earlier. Cocky reckoned the law would never think he'd try and use the same method of shipment. What he didn't realise was that a little birdie had already told the Old Bill that Cocky was about to pull off this Charlie deal.

Cocky dreamt up a scheme to import the drugs to Bulgaria through his 'wine interests'. The coke would be cooked into liquid and – here's the clever bit – then held in suspension inside bottles of Bulgarian red plonk. Then it would be shipped back across Europe to Warren's beloved Merseyside where it would be banged out at a 2,000 per cent mark-up.

First the Charlie turned up at Cocky's Dutch hacienda in a container filled with those lead ingots. That's when Holland's version of the SAS moved in with stun grenades and busted

Cocky and his team. Moments after the Dutch SWAT team smashed down his front door, they found Cocky in bed with a busty Ukranian hooker.

Many hours of drilling holes in metal ingots followed before more than 400 kilos of pure Colombian marching powder was uncovered. At six other addresses lived in by Warren's mates, Dutch police found millions of pounds' worth of other drugs and enough weaponry to start a civil war. By the time they'd counted it all up, the Dutch cops reckoned they'd bagged £125 million worth of drugs.

Cocky Warren's trial in Holland was even switched at short notice to a secret location after Dutch police got wind of a plan to spring Cocky from jail. The change in venue was so sudden it left dozens of British reporters watching proceedings on a screen in the Paleis Van Justitie. At first the Dutch authorities refused to say where the trial was to be conducted. Cocky had provoked a lot of fear and trepidation.

When the trial finally got under way, Cocky denied six charges relating to specific quantities of drugs and to the illegal possession of firearms. The most serious charge was that Cocky had masterminded the trafficking operation from his mansion in Sassenheim. His two old mates from the UK, Stephen Mee and Stephen Whitehead, stood with him in the dock.

At one stage proceedings were halted after claims that evidence against Cocky 'may have been contaminated'. His brief

Han Jahae claimed that British investigators had illegally tapped into Cocky's phones rendering the Dutch prosecution null and void. Jahae also insisted that evidence used against Cocky in that early Newcastle trial, in which he had been acquitted, should not be used in this latest case.

Cocky was even allowed to issue a statement after the Dutch judge adjorned the case while four extra witnesses were located. He told reporters, 'It's important that you investigate how the English got their information. Why did they need to claim public immunity?'

Cocky finally copped a 12-year stretch in Holland and the judge made a point of telling the court that he had not given him the maximum 16-year sentence because Warren did not belong to 'the extremely violent drugs barons'. Many would no doubt disagree with that statement. Cocky wasn't in court for his sentencing but he'd already dismissed the charges against him as being 'a police set-up'.

Britain's Customs and Excise put on a brave face. 'An entire drugs gang has been destroyed,' said Paul Acda, deputy chief. 'Warren was a unique trafficker in British terms, because he had direct contact with the sources of the drugs. It will take a long time before anybody takes his place.'

Cocky knew he would have received double the sentence back in Britain although the police in Britain concede it would have been a nightmare trying to find a jury who wouldn't have ended up being intimidated by Cocky's pals. And don't forget that some of his closest mates also happened to be members of the constabulary.

Even from his prison cell, however, Cocky Warren continued to have his finger in a lot of pies. He's boasted of owning Barrow Football Club's ground. They're in the Conference League. The police believe he's also invested heavily in a number of football league clubs. And the Football Association have even helped the Customs and police with their enquiries into Cocky's activities.

The National Crime Squad spent many months probing Cocky's links with Stephen Vaughan, Barrow FC's former chairman and owner who resigned in late 1998. While there's no suggestion that Vaughan was connected to any of Cocky's criminal activities there was concern about Cocky using some of his millions to keep the club afloat.

Vaughan bought the club in 1995 and was widely credited with saving it from going down the pan. But 18 months later he was questioned about his links to Cocky Warren and claims that the club had been fraudulently purchased. Vaughan admits knowing Cocky, but insists that's only because he had at one time employed Warren's security company for his boxing promotions.

Vaughan also admitted, 'He [Warren] once put £17,500 into my solicitor's account to buy a council house I wanted to sell, but the deal never went through and I gave him his money back. I did buy a Toyota Land Cruiser from him.'

Recently, there were rumours in Merseyside that Cocky Warren and a consortium of associates were trying to buy a controlling stake in one of the first division's top sides. But after the club heard about the Curtis Warren connections they refused to meet the group of 'businessmen'. Cocky was so narked by the club's attitude that he's now even more determined to target a top club. One of his former associates recently explained, 'Cocky sees soccer as the ultimate ego trip. He wants to control a club because he likes the idea of the powerbase and it is also a great way to launder a lot of dirty money.'

During the police investigation into Cocky's links to certain football clubs, they launched a separate inquiry into his father-in-law Philly Glennon, nicknamed the Silver Fox. They believed that he'd also made a fortune out of drug dealing. When Merseyside detectives paid a recent visit to Glennon's home they found more than £1 million in cash buried in his back garden. Glennon was described at the trial of Cocky's favourite bent cop as a 'wealthy crook who made his money through drugs'.

The police even discovered that an off-shore company gave one football club connected to Cocky a £300,000 loan even though the company did not appear to have ever traded. Police also unearthed evidence that cash from drugs deals had been laundered through a bunch of property transactions involving an investment company based in the Isle of Man.

Cocky first came up with the idea of taking over a football club after visiting his Cali cartel cronies in Colombia, where drug barons moved into the soccer business years ago. In one notorious incident the cartel shot national team defender Andrs Escobar after he scored an own goal in the World Cup finals.

Meanwhile, Cocky was banged up in the maximum security prison at Vught, on the site of a former Nazi concentration camp in Holland. During the first few months after he was sent down, other inmates said he was a quiet prisoner steering clear of trouble. He knew that outside those four walls dozens of cops were working round the clock to track down his tens of millions of pounds. When Customs officials got wind of rumours that at least £10 million of Cocky's money had been secretly deposited in a Swiss bank account he shrugged his shoulders and told one associate, 'It's a small price to pay.'

But Cocky's influence continued to reach far beyond the bars of his Dutch prison cell. Greater Manchester police nicked one of their own officers shortly after Cocky's incarceration and accused him of helping the megawealthy gangster to launder millions of pounds in drugs cash.

Back in Merseyside the run-down streets remained paved in gold thanks to Cocky and his team of dealers and suppliers. Amid many boarded-up shops, deserted streets and the faded grandeur of a bygone era there are bizarre pockets of immense wealth in Liverpool; flashy nightclubs; designer clothes shops. Official statistics suggest a city on the edge of financial ruin. But out on the streets, Cocky is considered a Robin Hood-style hero who's provided vast salaries for hundreds of people feeding off the massive profits of drug dealing.

Flashy limos cruise the streets and virtually every kid on a street corner seems to own a mobile. Even the much respected *North-West Business Insider*, a regional business magazine, recently declared drugs were behind most of the city's small business success stories. It's reckoned Warren's team are still shifting 500kg of drugs each and every month.

Just have a think about this statistic: a police raid on a ship in Rotterdam recently uncovered 800kg worth of Charlie with a street value of £75 million. In other words, that 500kg is worth at least £46 million a month – big money in anyone's terms.

And Cocky's empire had long since spread to London, the Midlands and Scotland. As Steve Brauner, editor of *North-West Business Insider*, says, 'He's like a broker in legal commodities. He negotiates a price with the suppliers – in this case the Colombian cocaine cartel – before selling on several slices of the consignment at a mark-up to other criminal organisations. The profit on those deals mean he's getting the rest of the consignment for nothing. His profit on any drugs brought into this country is 100 per cent.'

GANGS OF BRITAIN

Last summer, 2000, Cocky's team ordered a steady stream of travellers clutching sports bags to board buses and trains from Liverpool to London. Mingling with tourists, they then exchanged cash sums as high as £500,000 at Bureaux de Change in the capital. Much of it was changed into large denomination notes of Dutch gilders or German marks. That money was then carefully banked in offshore tax havens. The couriers from Liverpool are bunged £300 a time for their journey south. They'd never dare to do a runner with the loot. 'It's more than their life's worth,' says one who knows.

Cocky's biggest problem has always been to get the money back from his offshore accounts to Merseyside. In recent years he's cracked that problem by backing small businesses with loans. The father of one of Warren's police mates even helped him set up a string of small companies which appeared to lack any income yet held money in the bank. Cocky naturally kept his name out of all documentation. There's no Inland Revenue record, nor has he ever claimed any benefit. Even the fancy mansion he still owns out in posh Hoylake, north of Liverpool, was bought in the name of a dead man with no dependants.

His numerous terraced houses in Liverpool appear to belong to a respectable property company – except that it is in receipt of a mysterious offshore loan for £2 million and no one will say who lent them the money. Cocky's never been too keen on paperwork. Before he was banged up in Holland he'd turn up at companies he wanted to 'invest' in with a bag of readies usually stuffed with at least £500,000. There were never any papers to sign so nothing could link Cocky to his business loans scheme.

So, while Cocky continues serving his time, back in Liverpool the gangs who virtually blasted each other to oblivion in the mid-1990s don't even dare to try and reclaim Cocky's turf. He's been above such local difficulties for years and no one will cross him. Yet ironically, Cocky had been trying to broker a peace deal between warring Jamaicans and other street dealers when he got sent down by the court in Holland.

The Merseyside police effort to carve up Cocky's territory and break the other drug cartels in Liverpool looks doomed to failure. Customs officers have even been forced to base their own investigation at least 30 miles outside the city for their own safety. Customs planning raids have been told by local cops they cannot guarantee their safety. Despite being heavily armed and carefully targeting specific gangters they know that any unknown motor near a villain's house on Merseyside will be spotted by kids with mobile phones, often supplied by Cocky's team.

In June 1999, Cocky launched an appeal against his Dutch prison sentence. His lawyers insisted British security officers illegally passed on info to the Dutch police. They even claimed they could win a retrial in front of a new judge and threatened to take the case to the European Court of Human Rights.

Then in September 1999, Cocky found it wasn't so easy being banged up after all. He got himself into some heavy-duty aggro which ended up with him flooring a mad Turk who came at him with a knife and a head butt. The poor bastard ended up dead after Cocky lashed out with a couple of killer punches.

Guards at the prison insisted Cocky was first headbutted by his fellow inmate, 37-year-old Turkish cellmate Gema Guclu. Curtis then punched him back and within seconds they were hitting out and kicking each other and rolling over on the ground. Screws quickly cleared other prisoners out of their cells and into a secure unit, ignoring Cocky's deadly bare-knuckle dust-up. They later said it would have been too dangerous to separate the men fighting while other prisoners were 'in the immediate vicinity'.

A Dutch Justice Ministry spokewoman said, 'When the guards returned they saw Curtis Warren standing over the other man, who was lying on the ground, obviously badly injured.' The Turk was rushed to hospital and put on a life support machine, but he died the following day from a brain haemorrhage.

For months officials wouldn't confirm whether the con died as a result of being hit by Cocky or whether his haemorrhage was caused by the Turk head-butting Cocky! Cocky's Manchester-based brief Keith Dyson said at the time, 'My client was attacked in the prison yard. There were no weapons involved and we hope it was picked up on CCTV cameras.' He insisted that Cocky's appeal against his Dutch prison sentence would still go ahead.

On 16 November 1999, Cocky's appeal was turned down. His lawyers insisted they would take the case to the European court of human rights.

But Cocky, who's always prided himself on keeping his operation low key, was even more upset when he found out in March 2000 that a book about his criminal career had just been published. *Cocky* (Milo Books, £14.99) spells out a lot of Warren's ducking and diving and presses home the point that the man himself has managed to hold on to most of his vast fortune. 'Cocky's not happy about the book because it winds up the British authorities who are still hunting for all his hidden cash,' says one old Merseyside associate.

The police themselves are still scratching their nuts trying to get a whiff of the really big money. 'Who fuckin' knows where he's stashed it? We reckon most of it's gone to somewhere like Dubai and from there it's in a black hole,' says one frustrated cop. Cocky was also well narked about the book describing him as being nothing more than a street-level dealer in the late Eighties, 'a nobody on the first rung of the ladder'.

Meanwhile his first big backer – 'The Banker' – is now in semi-retirement in Brussels. In early 2000, the then Home Secretary Jack Straw referred to a drugs baron who had amassed a £450 million fortune and was one of the richest people in Britain. When a friend of The Banker asked if Straw had been talking about him, he replied, 'Well, I don't think so, but I'm not sure.'

Cocky is undoubtedly still in possession of a fortune reckoned to be in the region of £200 million. British Customs officers and police are working with the Dutch to try and grab some of that dirty dosh but they'll be lucky if they trace a tenth of what Warren owns.

Naturally, Cocky continues to claim he was fitted up by the Customs men in tandem with the Dutch police. He also insists he only owns a couple of modest houses in Liverpool and that rumours of his incredible wealth have been greatly exaggerated.

But Cocky remains one of Britain's richest gangsters. His money is stashed in tax havens and Swiss bank accounts. He's still got a penthouse apartment in Liverpool's swanky Wapping Dock development. Then there are the office blocks he's invested in, plus those 200 properties in the north west of England, mainly let out to DSS claimants.

There's also that detached eight-bedroom mansion tucked away in Hoylake on the Wirral, outside Liverpool. Then there's the villa in Holland, a couple of casinos in Spain and a disco in Turkey.

In a nutshell, Cocky Warren has virtually single-handedly turned Liverpool into the hub of the British drugs trade. He remains so powerful that he can stop supplies going to anyone who crosses him.

* * *

ENDNOTE

In January 2001, the cops finally had a bit of a result in their bid to nab Cocky's loot when he was forced to hand over £5 million to avoid another five years in the slammer in Holland. Cocky, now 37, was well upset when his lawyers informed him that under Dutch law anyone convicted of a crime and suspected of profiting from it could be forced to serve time in the nick if they couldn't prove how they got the money.

Warren handed over the cash after Customs officers travelled to Holland to give evidence to Dutch authorities. The £5 million is the largest sum ever seized in Holland. The evidence included references to four properties on Merseyside plus a large amount of dosh which briefs insist was owned by Cocky. Investigators also said he owned 270 terraced houses in the North West of England plus other businesses spread across Europe.

The Old Bill continue trying to track down more of Cocky's fortune, although privately they admit they don't hold out much hope. As one British Customs investigator said recently, 'It's a pig's ear of a system. The law as it stands favours the drug baron. We have to find the money first. Society just isn't serious about tackling hard drugs.'

And they say crime doesn't pay!

FINAL ENDNOTE

Cocky got an extra four years on his sentence for the killing of Gema Guclu following a special Dutch prison hearing on 24 February 2001. Cocky insisted he was simply defending himself when he kicked and punched his Turkish cellmate to death. Following the sentencing, Cocky said through his brief, 'I regret the man dying but I was just defending myself.'

CHAPTER

4

JIMMY MOODY
O.B.E.

'I'm not ashamed of my dad, because
he did what he did for his own
reasons. All I know is he'd be proud
I didn't turn out like him.'

MOODY'S SON JASON.

Combine the Kray Twins with the Richardsons and a sprinkling of the Guv'nor Lenny McLean, plus an IRA hitman thrown in for good measure, and you start to get an idea of Jimmy Moody's underworld credentials. And as they say in gangland Britain: 'He may be dead but his spirit lives on. Moody's career spanned more than four decades and included run-ins with Jack Spot, Billy Hill, 'Mad' Frankie Fraser, the Krays, the Richardsons and the Provos.

James Alfred Moody was number one enforcer for the Richardsons, did freelance 'work' for the Krays and became probably the most feared gangster ever to emerge from the London underworld – all before he reached thirty years of age. And just like the Krays he even worshipped his dear old mum.

Moody's first starring role came when he survived one of South London's most legendary club battles at a venue called Mr Smith's and the Witchdoctor's, a cabaret and gambling house in Catford in the early 1960s. Fighting broke out around 3.30 a.m., when a small-time hood and Krays sidekick called Dickie Hart started waving a piece around and shot another villain called Henry Rawlings. Hart was plugged on the spot. Then all hell broke lose and Jimmy Moody ended up carrying the wounded, including Charlie Richardson and Frankie Fraser, out of the club before disappearing in a cloud of smoke. He was later acquitted of any involvement in the shootings.

Some reckon the battle inside Mr Smith's was deliberately engineered by the Krays who wanted to dismantle the

Richardson's powerbase. As James Morton says in his book *Gangland Britain*, 'This was an attempt by the Krays – with whom the Richardsons were, at the time, in serious disagreement over the rights to provide security for a blue-film racket in the West End – to dispose of their rivals once and for all.'

Then Jimmy Moody's reputation got another boost in 1967 when he was convicted of manslaughter over the death of a young merchant navy steward called William Day. Moody copped a six-stretch for that little number. In the clink Moody became a committed body builder and on his release joined a notorious band of armed robbers known as the Chainsaw Gang which specialised in hijacking security vans in south east London.

Moody was a quiet, reserved sort of fellow who tended to stand back on the edge of a crowd. But at this time his bosses the Richardsons encountered numerous showbusiness stars including Barbara Windsor's ex-hubby Ronnie Knight and even Frank Sinatra during their visits Up West. And all this time, Moody hung back in the shadows keeping an eye on things.

What none of those celebs realised was that Jimmy Moody was already a contract killer at a time when even the phrase was virtually unknown. As such he was a vital member of the Richardsons' inner circle. Moody was their official 'enforcer' – a godfather, feared and respected by the London underworld.

One time, Moody, dressed as a copper, jumped out of a motor in the Blackwall Tunnel and forced a security van to stop.

To prevent anyone raising the alarm he leaned into nearby cars and lobbed their keys into the gutter. In 1980, Moody found himself on the run from the law after yet another hijack when he visited a relative's flat in Brixton and was nicked for a series of blaggings involving a massive total of £930,000.

He was then locked up in Brixton on remand. In those days it was still possible for inmates awaiting trial to have food, wine and beer brought in by friends and relatives. One Sunday lunchtime Moody's brother Richard brought in hacksaw blades, drill bits and other tools. Within days Moody, his cellmate IRA bomber Gerard Tuite and Stanley Thompson, a veteran of the Parkhurst Prison riots of 1969 and now banged up on an armed robbery charge, had begun cutting their way through the brickwork. On December 16 1980, they pushed out the loosened masonry of their cell, stepped onto a roof where a ladder had been left by workmen and were on their toes. Tuite and Moody vanished while Thompson was soon run to ground.

But Moody's story only took on legendary proportions because of what happened to him after he went on the run from Brixton Prison. It turned out that Moody's cellmate Tuite had told him countless tales of brutality and torture inflicted by the British across the water. Moody even looked a touch Irish with his heavy build, thick black eyebrows and bulldog neck. Mind you, others reckon Moody earned £10,000 by helping Tuite go over the wall from Brixton. Anyway, across the water, Moody's murderous skills were soon put to good use by the Provos. He became their secret deadly assassin – a man who struck so much fear into Northern Ireland's security services that at one stage in the mid-1980s the Thatcher Government assigned a special three-man hit-team of crack SAS men to finish him off.

It was then Moody coined the most chilling gangster-fuelled phrase of all time when he began referring to his victims as having been awarded an 'O.B.E.' (One Behind the Ear). It went on to become the calling card used by many Belfast killers over the following 15 years. Meanwhile, Moody had fine-tuned his skills as a hitman and become the number one hired killer on both sides of the water. He was even renowned for professionally disposing of his victims' bodies if that was part of the contract or making sure that death occured in a public place as a 'message' to others.

But, believe it or not, there was a human, caring side to this cold-blooded killer. While on the run in Ireland, Moody desperately missed his wife Val and their two kids back in Dulwich, South London. The cozzers almost nicked him in London when he flew in for a reunion with his son. He only got away when a bent copper tipped him the nod and he scarpered minutes before a posse of the local Old Bill swooped.

And in the middle of all this, Moody even deliberately fed informers, including the British security services, with inaccurate information which enabled him to survive on the run for more years than anyone else with the exception of Ronnie Biggs.

But back in Belfast, Jimmy Moody was pissing off some of his IRA paymasters by hopping in and out of bed with local brasses on virtually a daily basis. On a number of occasions he slept with women who were working as informants for the British Government, but somehow Moody escaped the long arm of the law. Not surprisingly, some Provos started to consider him a bloody liability.

By the late 1980s, Moody knew full well that he was in danger of overstaying his welcome on the Emerald Isle. The lure of the East End and all his old mates persuaded Moody to return to the smoke. He was convinced that his reputation as a hired killer would keep him one step ahead of trouble – and the law.

But the London he returned to was a very different place from the one he'd left ten years earlier. Huge drug deals – usually involving Ecstasy and cocaine – were financing many criminals' lavish lifestyles instead of armed robbery. The stakes were higher and so were the profits. Even a hardened soul like Jimmy Moody was disturbed by what he saw. He warned his own children to steer clear of drugs. But then he was renowned as a man who would not even tolerate other people smoking in his company.

However Moody still had to earn a crust and, in the middle of all this, it's rumoured he knocked off one or two of the most notorious faces in London. They'd got up the noses of their drug baron mates big time. Moody knew that his reputation as a real hardman had to be maintained in the face of all these multi-millionaire drug barons. Other people's deaths once again became his main source of income. In 1990, the cozzers named him as the chief suspect in the 'plugging' of a member of one notorious south London criminal family. And Moody never denied his involvement. However, he told one old-time gangster that he knew he never should have taken the job because that family had never done him harm in the past and now they were after his blood. 'Jimmy knew he'd made a mistake and that he might end up paying the ultimate price for topping that geezer,' explained the south east London villain.

Some old-time faces still believe to this day that Moody continued being an informant to the Met because he reckoned it would help him stay on the run. He's rumoured by some to have provided the cozzers with information which led to the nicking of some of those involved in the Brink's-Mat gold bullion raid at Heathrow Airport in 1984. If this is true it is sensational news because it means that Moody was helping the Met while he was popping people in Northern Ireland on behalf of the Provos.

Soon after the plugging of that member of the south London crime family in 1990, Moody told his ex-wife he wanted to turn over a new leaf and retire from the gangsterdom before it was too late. He always defended himself in public by insisting he never once killed an innocent person. 'Each and every one of them deserved what they got, they were toerags,' he told one old mate. But try telling that to the families and friends of his victims …

Anyway, Moody got himself a job managing a pub in a quiet Essex village. He had a new name, a new bit of crumpet and life seemed almost sweet. But it didn't last long; he had to quit when an old face walked into that boozer and put the finger on him. Then Moody landed himself another job pulling pints, this time at a pub in Walworth, slap bang in the middle of his old manor. Even though he prided himself on keeping a low profile, he believed he was better off amongst his own.

As another old-timer later explained, 'You got more chance of surviving on home territory. There's always someone to let you know the cozzers are sniffing around or a face from another manor is on your tail. It makes total sense.'

But by this time – the early 1990s – Jimmy Moody's list of enemies read like a Who's Who of criminal faces from across both sides of the water. There was also the police, the RUC and the British security services. It was only a matter of time before someone's barrel pointed in his direction.

Moody was now known as 'Mick the Irishman' and that clock was still ticking away until he finally got awarded his own O.B.E. That 'gong' came on the night of 1 June 1993 while 'Mick' was drinking at the bar of the Royal Hotel in Hackney. Three bullets to the head and one to the back from a hitman special – a .38 revolver just like Moody's favourite weapon of choice. It was a cruel epitaph.

The fellow who shot Moody was in his early forties wearing a leather bomber jacket. The shooter had even first ordered his own pint of Foster's lager and put two coins down on the bar to pay for it. Then he turned towards Moody and carried on blasting away as he slumped to the floor. The killer scarpered in a stolen Ford Fiesta that was sat revving up outside the boozer driven by an accomplice.

As Moody's son, Jason, an actor, told one reporter at the time: 'I'm not ashamed of my dad, because he did what he did for his own reasons. All I know is he'd be proud I didn't turn out like him.'

At the time of his demise, Jimmy Moody had been living in Wadeson Street, a back alley off Mare Street, in Hackney. Some reckoned that Moody was topped because he was banging someone's missus. Others pointed the finger at a power-struggle between our old friends the Arifs and the Brindles. Then there was the IRA and the British security services.

Just after his death, Moody was conveniently linked to a number of other killings, including that of Terry Gooderham and his girlfriend Maxine Arnold in Epping Forest in December 1989 plus antique and cocaine dealer Peter Rasini in Palmers Green in March 1991. Moody was also fancied for the plugging of Peter and Gwenda Dixon, whose bodies were found near an arms cache in 1989.

Mad Frankie Fraser in his book *Mad Frank* has another take on Jimmy Moody's demise: 'It now turns out that Jimmy Moody was working in a pub at the back of Walworth. He'd been in the area for ten years. He wasn't an out-and-out nightclubber so he could have been there and very, very few people would know who he was. He's done quite a bit of bird and now he took it as a personal thing to keep out. It was a personal challenge for him.

He could be stubborn and obstinate, a good man but a loner. He'd be content to do his work and watch the telly knowing that every day was a winner. That's how he would look at it.'

Meanwhile the mother of the one of Moody's most recent victims said, 'I'm glad Moody's dead. My family is overjoyed. The police rang to tell us this morning. He got it the way he gave it out. I'm glad he didn't die straight away. That man was evil and I hope he rots in hell.'

Jimmy Moody was a unique modern-day gangster whose activities have had an ominous knock-on effect on Britain's criminal underworld to this day. His illegal activities covered the whole spectrum, including using so-called modern crimes such as stalking, serial killing and road rage as a disguise for the perfect hit. In many ways, Jimmy Moody perfectly encapsulated the archetypal London criminal. But he always wanted more, and that inevitably incurred the wrath of numerous gangsters and, as we now know, even members of the Provisional IRA. So it was no surprise that a price was put on his head.

Jimmy Moody pulled no punches. His life revolved around violence, black humour, the bizarre and the unemotional. But he was prepared to go beyond those traditional boundaries in order to make his name in the underworld. Murder was the recurring theme of Jimmy Moody's turbulent life. He admitted to at least a dozen murders, and if you live by the sword you eventually will die by it …

CHAPTER
5

JOSIE DALY

'Good luck to the girls, I say.
They make a fortune. I'm happy
with what comes through the till.
Everyone does well. Even my
receptionist can earn £100 a day
with tips from the girls.'

JOSIE DALY

Josie Daly, sharp as a knife and ten times more cunning, has been servicing punters as London's most powerful madam for almost 30 years. Today the 64-year-old brothel keeper is one of the richest women in Britain. She lives in a seven-bedroom mansion called Bunty's Corner named after her dearly departed favourite Alsatian. She's got a Roller in the driveway and her vice business has earned her more than £10 million.

Josie's palace in North London is her pride and joy. She's even spent a fortune getting artists to paint pictures of her favourite pets on to the stain-glassed porch window panes. Photos of beloved Bunty, her brother Crunchy and Sammy-poo, an Alsatian-Dalmatian cross, dominate the walls of Josie's home in Crouch End. All three of them are dead now, buried in the garden with plaques and dog statues to mark their graves.

But there's another side to Josie that's summed up by the secure iron gate arrangement halfway down the hall of her house that can be slammed shut and locked in seconds. Good security is essential in Josie's game because her team are in the habit of dropping £10,000 in cash into the house at any time of the day or night.

Josie bought the house for cash eight years ago and the first thing she did was splash out tens of thousands on building a twelve-foot-high black and gold electronic fence around the whole gaff. In the driveway her pristine white Roller lies under a tarpaulin just in case it ever gets any dust on it.

Josie's also got a few other properties scattered around town; there's a hostel in nearby Crouch End, where hookers used to stay, plus two other hotels – one in Muswell Hill and a 60-bedroom flophouse nearby which grew so tatty she had to close it down. But its value has been going up at the rate of £5,000 a week thanks to London's property boom of recent years.

One former member of her staff, a pretty brunette with long legs, reckons Josie's a brothel keeper with a heart of gold. 'She never made us feel like shit and we all knew what we were getting ourselves into. I won't hear a word against her. Josie's the tops.'

These days Josie spends a lot of her time shuffling across a thick, pink shagpile in her lounge that would put Liberace to shame. Her two beloved mutts, 11-year-old Mezchal and three-year-old Fifi love nuzzling up to their mistress. Her favourite armchair is covered in her favourite colours, black and gold. But her favourite possession is … cash. 'I love it. I live for it. It's my life,' she says to this day.

Yet despite her millions, Josie rarely leaves the capital. She hasn't had a holiday in more than 25 years. She says she'll never leave London and it's her life. And London certainly knows Josie – especially the local cozzers and the courts of justice. Josie reckons she has a reputation to maintain and just to prove it before a recent case she bunged a mate a few bob to produce a glossy press release professing her innocence. In it she claimed that sickness had prevented her from stopping her massage parlours providing more services than British Telecom. 'When I was in good health, I stamped out any illegal activity, sacking any girls associated with it.' Really, Josie?

But then Josie's fancy mansion sitting atop Crouch End is a far cry from her humble roots in southern Ireland. Born in the village of Ardangeehy, County Cork, she was the youngest of eight children. Her parents, Jack and Eileen, ran a smallholding and struggled to feed their kids. 'We had cows and a couple of ponies, pigs and chickens,' says Josie. 'I wasn't very good at school and left at 15 with no qualifications. But when I was older I was good at whatever I did.'

That's when Josie headed across the water to stay with a sister called Margaret in Bournemouth. She became a student nurse. Then Josie, a real looker in those days, started knocking off a handsome young student doctor from Bournemouth. The couple had a daughter, Emelia Tawaih. Her only child, now in her thirties, has remained loyally by her mum's side ever since.

A few years later, Josie moved to London where she trained in tissue studies at Paddington Technical College. A spell working at a clinic that treated baldness followed. Not long after that Josie fell into the London massage parlour game. She has a rose-tinted recollection of those good old days. 'I worked at a hospital with a nice young man called John who had a woman friend called Anne who ran a massage business. We were talking about it one day and I was due some holidays so I went to help her run the place. It was very, very busy there and I was getting paid and I started saving.'

Josie ended up running that sauna for a year before branching out on her own. She even reckons she took a massage course along the way which later helped her 'spot the women coming to work for the wrong reason'.

By the early 1980s she was pulling in a small fortune. 'The clients were lovely. We'd sit and chat for hours.' Then in 1992 Josie says she suffered a massive heart attack and began taking a 'less active role' in the business which now had three 'branches' – all in the Camden area. Josie briefly owned another establishment as well before selling it on. The local cops had her labelled as 'a premiership' brothel keeper.

Josie even ran a massage training centre, which provided girls with NVQ qualifications. She also owned another house where many of the girls would stay. Josie made a crust out of that operation as well, by charging them rent.

Girls worked in Josie's four brothels around the clock on 12-hour shifts and up to one thousand geezers came through her premises each six-day week seeking out some of Josie's renowned 'extras'. Josie took a minimum £10 cut from each and every one.

The only time she had a problem with her girls was when she employed a fella in drag by mistake. 'This girl was really lovely with blonde hair and nice boobs,' she later explained. 'But I didn't realise it was a bloke waiting for a sex change until some clients rang up and told me I'd employed a man. I had to ask him to leave.'

Then in 1992 the good old *News of the Screws* took a pop at Josie and turned her over in a splash article headlined 'Cops and Brothels,' which exposed some of her most valuable customers as being ... the Old Bill! The tabloid even uncovered that Josie was employing a former CID chief to do her books. That same silly old plod had fixed up two hookers for the paper's undercover investigator posing as a punter.

The ex-cop even encouraged Josie to advertise her vice business in police magazines. The *News of the Screws* then got hold of a letter signed by him which confirmed that he had been 'a very close friend' of Josie Daly for the previous 20 years.

But then Josie always handpicked her staff and confidants with great care. Her grown-up daughter, Emelia, regularly helps out on the reception of her massage parlours. When Josie was turned over by the tabloids she even boasted to one reporter disguised as a punter, 'The police need a massage too, you know. I was even invited to a CID Christmas ball. I took a bottle of whisky and a bottle of brandy, but I didn't stay. It was too noisy for me.'

Josie, then married to a retired GP from Wolverhampton, also told the undercover hack, 'Good luck to the girls, I say. They make a fortune. I'm happy with what comes through the till. Everyone does well. Even my receptionist can earn £100 a day with tips from the girls.'

* * *

For more than 20 years Josie kept the Old Bill at arm's length thanks to greasing the right palms and making sure all the right movers and shakers got exactly what they wanted when it came to a bit of the old slap and tickle. Josie gainfully employed more than 50 women, aged between 18 and 30, many from Britain and Eastern Europe and the Far East in her operation and she took home a fortune in anyone's terms. Josie was in the habit of dropping in unannounced at her premises in her chauffeur-driven white Roller just to make sure all the usual services were being provided.

Then the cops launched a crackdown and undercover police posing as customers were met by receptionists who handed them a menu listing a choice of sauna, steam and massage. After paying £10 or £15 to the receptionist, customers were handed a towel and invited to take a shower before being asked to choose a girl. Then a range of sexual services were offered as 'extras', costing another £15 to £50.

Josie only came unstuck when the cops discovered that some of her premises, licensed as massage and sauna parlours by the local council in Camden, didn't even have a sauna! They also reckoned she'd been hiring girls smuggled into Britain by illegal immigrant traffickers.

The boys in blue traced the ownership of the massage parlours to Josie's home in Crouch End. They watched staff pick up keys there every morning and they spotted bags of cash were taken from the premises to her mansion several times a day. Josie later admitted that there were also large sacks of rubbish deliberately dropped at the house to avoid arousing the suspicion of the local police. As DI Paul Holmes said, 'She was a significant player in the London prostitution racket.'

When Josie was finally nicked in the summer of 1999, a lot of faces reckoned she might blow the lid on some of her VIP client list which included politicians, celebrities and a bunch of top cops. Instead, Josie took to her wheelchair, admitted three counts of controlling prostitution and avoided a spell in the slammer by claiming she was at death's door. Some of Josie's rich and powerful clients even sent bouquets of flowers to Harrow Crown Court, North West London, where the case was heard. The court heard she had at least ten bank accounts. Some showed balances of up to £90,000. Another £104,500 was found in the bedroom of her prized mansion.

Josie was such a shrewd operator, however, she'd openly declared a turn-over of £250,000 for tax purposes. But as prosecutor Brendan Kelly told the court, 'This was simply a reflection of the aggregate of the receptionists' fees and made no account of the income received by the prostitutes.'

Naturally, the Old Bill insisted, 'This was a very, very profitable business. We had known about Josie Daly for some time, but didn't realise the scale of her operation.' Another policeman described her as a 'plausible raconteur' and 'a very controlling, exploitative woman'.

The court exercised its power to confiscate cash and assets amassed over the previous five years. Josie looked set to cop a figure as high as £7.5 million, based on £3 million that had been invested in property and £4.5 million that had passed through her bank accounts. But following a lengthy conflab between lawyers outside the court on the last day of her appearance, the prosecution agreed to a figure of £2 million because dear old Josie had been a good girl and paid all her VAT and income tax from her sex business. The judge even accepted that a third of her business was legit.

Giving her a year to cough up the cash or face five years inside, Judge Barrington Black said, 'The defendant has accepted she profited from the running of what has been described as a series of well-run and highly organised brothels. It is perfectly clear that the defendant was fully aware of what was going on.' But the judge wouldn't swallow Josie's supposed illness when she arrived in court in that wheelchair. He said he had 'misgivings' about her condition.

Outside the court Josie admitted that she still lived with her daughter in her £1 million mansion in Crouch End and still owned her white Roller. She also conceded that losing £2 million wouldn't make much difference to her five-star lifestyle. Josie reckoned she'd have to flog her three 'saunas' to pay the fine. But there was no way she'd part with her mansion – it was her pride and joy. There's no doubt that shrewd operator Josie still has a fortune stashed away somewhere. She's also not shy about mentioning that some of her best customers were members of the Met's top brass.

Irish-born and renowned for her use of the blarney, Josie told one keen young hack she'd be celebrating her escape from jail with a glass of the best champers, 'I'm glad the court allowed me to choose what properties to sell because it would have been awful to lose my house.' Josie also told anyone who would listen that she was retiring from the vice game. She insisted, 'I am afraid I will have to retire now because I can't start again. I never want to go through this again.' But as one local cop said later, 'Josie'll still have her finger in the game, if you know what I mean.'

Even Judge Barrington Black conceded, 'A woman can offer her body if she wants to. Prostitution, as we all know, has been going on forever. What the law cannot accept is that others, be they men or women, should profit by such an act.'

Josie still hoped she might get away with paying less. She said, 'I was hoping for £1 million which would have been easier to find, but I'll sort it. I don't want to go to prison. I don't think I would come out alive. As far as I'm concerned, I didn't know what the girls were up to. I was never there because of my ill-health. They did exactly what they liked.'

Throughout all this Josie continued to describe her brothels as 'highly respectable places visited by doctors, lawyers and bankers'. She added, 'We had a wide range of customers. Some of them had been coming for a long time.' Josie even made a point of saying how disgusted she was by the hundreds of used condoms found by the police when they'd raided her premises. But minutes later she boasted to one reporter, 'I know all my girls because I train them all. I like to take on girls who've never done it before. They're the best.'

By the time Josie was nicked in 1999 she'd paid off all the mortgages on at least half a dozen properties she owned and she intended to leave everything to her daughter.

In July 2000, the London *Evening Standard* splashed Josie's picture across the front page with a banner headline DOWNFALL OF THE £7 MILLION MADAM. As one of her associates later pointed out, 'Josie was laughing all the way to the bank when she read that one. She's got a fortune tucked away and they'll never find it.'

But there's another aspect to Josie's business acumen; she's provided a valuable service to geezers from all walks of life. 'Josie paid her tax like any normal, law-abiding citizen but she's been punished out of all proportion to the laws she allegedly broke,' one of her former girls said after Josie was exposed in the press.

Josie's always prided herself on her independence and she regularly saw off local faces who tried to muscle in on her business over the years. Josie Daly's name is well known to many of the gangsters mentioned in this book, especially the Adams family. 'But we left her alone 'cause she was a real pro and she had our respect,' says one North London face.

But now she's 'semi-retired' it's certain that ownership of her thriving business may be sold on to a team of local gangsters. At the time we went to press the word on the grapevine was that the Adams family were keeping a close eye on developments after hearing that a well-known East London family had moved in on Josie with an offer she was not expected to refuse.

Islington Council has already granted a new licence to one of Josie's old saunas and Haringey council has received a new application to run another. Islington Council confirmed that one of the saunas, the Aqua, had been licensed to Demetrios Athanasiou, a 48-year-old builder who gave two ages and two different addresses in Companies House records.

As one of her former girls recently explained, 'The cops have really blown it. They've turned over Josie and forced her to retire which has meant that a heavy family from East London has now taken over what had been a well-run, crime-free business. The stupid Old Bill have created more problems than they've solved.'

No doubt the law knows full well that Josie's knocking shops are still operating. Nothing's changed except the gentle, girl-run vice world created by Josie Daly has been replaced by East Londoners hellbent on squeezing every penny of profit out of the premises.

CHAPTER
6

'LA PATRONA' (LADY BOSS)

'I'd love to know how she went from the girl I knew to this monster. I know she wanted a better life but I can't believe she chose to get it through drugs and murder.'

HER FIRST HUBBY.

ROYAL BELGRAVE HOUSE, VICTORIA, CENTRAL LONDON, OCTOBER 1998

Dawn was still an hour away as eight black-clad figures armed with semi-automatic shooters crept on to the roof of one of London's poshest apartment blocks. Down on the street, another team was swarming through the back door of the building.

Minutes later, the SWAT teams of armed police burst in through the front door of Colombian cocaine cartel boss Luisa Bolivar's luxury flat just as the other mob abseiled down from the roof. They were taking no chances after being warned that Luisa – known as La Patrona (Lady Boss) – kept weapons on the premises and could well be accompanied by armed minders.

Luisa Bolivar has earned millions and lived a life of luxury in London that includes that £500-a-week apartment overlooking the Thames, a driver and limo to take her to £100-a-head restaurants and all the best designer clothes stores. And it's all down to her role as chief supplier of Colombia's finest marching powder to many of the city's richest residents. This beautiful 37-year-old drug baroness is a member of one of Colombia's most powerful drug cartels. She's made a fortune running a vast network of couriers bringing Charlie into Britain.

The petite, dark-haired Latina temptress Luisa brought murder and mayhem to the streets of London when one of her fellow South Americans showed disrepect to her handsome drug baron lover. As London DS Richard Blackwell says, 'She spent her time drinking champagne in clubs. She worked for the Colombian drug cartels. If she hadn't made one stupid mistake she'd still be out there making a fortune.'

Luisa Bolivar's transformation from the prim, naive teenager who arrived in London in 1978 to a manicured, sophisticated 37-year-old drug baroness was incredible. Back in the late seventies she'd been a penniless cleaner who told everyone she'd escaped Colombia because of its drugs and violence. She married her first husband, Frank Fleming, within a short time of arriving in London and told him she wanted to be a lawyer.

Ex-husband Fleming, 55, was later stunned to find out that in five short years Luisa had risen through the ranks to become one of the most powerful Colombian cartel operators in Europe. 'When I was married to her she was pure as the driven snow. Butter wouldn't melt in her mouth. She didn't smoke, drink or even swear. She was a real lady and had such high principles.'

Her ex-hubby also recalled, 'She told me she came here because she didn't want to live in a country with drugs, violence and killings. She hated drugs more than anything else. She had a passion against it, because she had seen what they had done to people back home. She is one of the nicest people I have met. She had perfect manners and was well-educated and bright. She was a grafter who went to bed early and got up early. It wasn't a marriage of convenience as such, but it was practical for both of us. She needed someone to look after her and I wanted the comfort. I am sure she liked the idea of being a British citizen as well.'

Luisa and her British hubby split up 15 months after the marriage. He admitted, 'I was drinking heavily and would come home late. She didn't like me doing that. I told her to leave if she wanted, so she did. We didn't keep in touch. I imagined her in a rich and successful job with a rich husband and a big house in the suburbs. I'd love to know how she went from the girl I knew to this monster. I know she wanted a better life but I can't believe she chose to get it through drugs and murder.' In fact, Luisa later married for the second time to a London-based Colombian called John Diaz and they had two children.

Luisa began her career with the coke cartels in the early Nineties when she was nicked for shoplifting in Tottenham and while awaiting trial was recruited by another inmate to work as a 'mule' for one of the cocaine gangs from her home city of Cali, the Charlie centre of the world. She was soon hiding drugs in her luggage or strapping them to her body. She proved a very cool customer and was quickly promoted. As one cop told me, 'Couriers were given £2,000 for every trip. It was a lucrative business.'

Then in 1994 Luisa was nicked with a cache of cocaine at Bogota's El Dorado airport. The couple had two daughters, now aged 18 and 13. Luisa served just nine months in prison after her coke cartel bosses were so impressed she hadn't grassed them up that they bunged the law some cash for her early release. Her two children had stayed in London with their father throughout her time behind bars.

Within days of Luisa's release she was back in London dating a debonair cartel boss called Juan-Carlos Fernandez, who went by the dual nicknames of 'Snake Hips' because of his love of dancing and 'Scarface' because of a knife attack on the streets of Cali. She'd even used her British passport gained through her first marriage to travel back to the UK. As one detective later explained, 'Things took off when she got together with Snake Hips. They were importing cocaine on a very large scale. Their income was enormous, but all illegal. She also made sure she was very hard to track down because she kept moving around.'

Luisa's work for the Cali cartel also included providing safe houses across London for illegal immigrants. But she didn't tell a soul in the capital that she'd just served time in a Colombian prison for that drug trafficking offence. Luisa remained one step ahead of the law by moving her henchmen and teams of couriers to different addresses on virtually a weekly basis.

On the surface, Luisa seemed a highly respectable member of the ever growing 60,000 official Colombian nationals living mostly in Central London. Many reckon another 20,000 are here illegally. 'And most of them are surviving by working for the drug cartels back home,' says one insider.

Many of these Colombian visitors travel into Britain as tourists and then 'disappear'. Others, as Luisa did 20 years ago, immediately seek out British men to marry. By the summer of 1996 Luisa had been promoted to recruiter and master smuggler for the Cali boys. Luisa hung out at some of the Colombian ex-pats' favourite haunts like La Bodeguita, a South American cafe in the Elephant and Castle shopping centre. It's filled with Colombian women with English surnames they've got through quick turn-round marriages.

Back in Cali, the Charlie boys elevated Luisa to the status of 'La Patrona' or lady boss. She had their respect and trust and they knew the streets of London were paved in millions. Soon Luisa was raking in around £50,000 a month. She bought at least three properties in London and even splashed out £15,000 on a Harley-Davidson motorcyle for her swarthy lover's birthday.

Then she rented that five-star gaff in Royal Belgrave House, Victoria, and coughed up six months' rent (£18,000) in advance in cash. She told friends she liked living in the best part of town and was happy to pay for that privilege. The other properties she owned continued to be rented out to homeless Colombians for rip-off rents which bagged her another fortune every week. Many of them were forced to work as drugs mules in order to pay for their rent.

Luisa – who stands just a shade over five feet when not in a pair of her favourite platforms – then began throwing her dosh in the direction of a London plastic surgeon. She shelled out tens of thousands of quid on liposuction for her stomach and hips. Then she had the wrinkles removed from under her eyes and she couldn't resist some breast enlargement.

So it was that the hugely reconstructed drugs baroness known as La Patrona found herself on Friday, 8 January 1998, at her favourite bar El Barco Latino, moored on the north side of the Thames near the Temple tube station. At one table on the crowded, floating nightclub sat 16-year-old Jorge Castillo, nicknamed Little Egg because of his shaven head, and several friends. At another table, Luisa was drinking with her drugs baron Latin lover Juan-Carlos Fernandez, the man with the double-barrelled nickname Snake Hips/Scarface.

A few minutes later a muscle-bound crony of Little Egg's called Yostin Ortiz accused Fernandez of touching him up – the worst slight in the macho Latin-American underworld. A fight broke out and Little Egg stupidly ripped the £500 gold chain from Fernandez's neck and ran off. The kid had only just escaped the slums of Bogota where both his parents had been topped in a feud between rival drug gangs.

La Patrona Luisa was furious at Little Egg's 'disrespect' to her powerful gangster lover. Fernandez drew his finger across his throat because he wanted the boy knocked off. Luisa had bought the gold chain for her steamy lover just a few days earlier. The next day she recruited hitman Hector Cedeno, 30, who'd just got back into Britain after serving time for cocaine possession and grievous bodily harm in New York. Cedeno slipped into Britain after flying into France and catching the Eurostar to Waterloo station. His documents weren't even checked.

Then, La Patrona called in 22-year-old Hernando Jaramillo, known as 'The Skunk' because he shaved his head with a blonde streak running down the middle resembling the tail of the animal. He was brought on board just to make sure Little Egg was taught a lesson he'd never forget. Luisa even had the scars on her lover's throat photographed so that Little Egg could be shown the picture before his own throat was squeezed. The Skunk had slipped into Britain pretending to be an asylum seeker. Back in Colombia, knocking off a street kid would hardly have warranted a police investigation so they weren't worried. Life's cheap on the streets of Cali.

Snake Hips/Scarface watched in admiration as his curvy Latin mistress organised the hit. Just hours before the killing was scheduled to take place, he slipped quietly out of Britain on a flight to Madrid, Spain.

Meanwhile Cedeno and The Skunk turned up at a south east London council flat where they knew Little Egg was staying. They asked him if he wanted to pop out with them to score some Charlie, which is the sort of thing Colombians do as frequently as the rest of us pop out for a pint. Little Egg was up for anything so he never even questioned their motives and skipped out to their waiting car, a borrowed VW Passat.

For more than an hour the three Colombians spun around the council estates of Lambeth and Brixton knocking up coke dealers, none of whom were in. Then the Passat turned into the Camberwell New Road and on to a notorious housing estate known to locals as 'Hell' where there had been a dozen shootings and at least three murders committed during the previous 12 months. They quickly scored a wrap of Charlie.

Then they parked the car up to share out the drugs. That's when ex-Colombian cop Cedeno – reputed to have knocked off dozens back home – leaned over from the back of the Passat and whipped a shoelace around the neck of Little Egg sitting in the front passenger seat. Cedeno wore white gloves as he expertly throttled the life out of the teenage tealeaf. The Skunk watched coldly and even rang La Patrona on his mobile to see if she wanted to listen to the youth take his last few breaths of life. As prosecutor Brian Altman later told the jury during a four-month trial, 'He pleaded as far as he could for his life. But he was shown no compassion.'

With the dead kid slumped on the passenger seat the two killers drove off laughing. That's when the Skunk called Luisa back to ask if she'd like Little Egg's ear or finger to prove the job had been done. She told them to dump Little Egg somewhere her people could inspect the corpse. A few minutes later his 5ft 3in, seven-and-a-half stone body was dropped in an industrial dustbin next to a children's playground.

That night Luisa's brother Diego was despatched to look at the body in the dumpster before giving the okay for the money to be paid. Meanwhile Cedeno went home to his flat at Tyler House, on the Stockwell Park Estate, in South Lambeth. The Skunk Jaramillo lived in Union Road, Clapham, south London. The brutal drug-fuelled Colombians had hit Britain's capital city with a vengeance.

The two hitmen then got a call from Diego saying he would hand over the first instalment of £2,000 the following day at a local tube station at one o'clock. Another £2,000 would be paid within a week. Cheap by anyone's standards.

But the exchange took place right under the nose of the local cozzers who were monitoring overhanging CCTV cameras for gangs of crackheads. The three Latinos were nicked for suspected drug dealing after the suitcase was opened. They were marched down to a copshop in nearby Belgravia where they were interrogated. Then Diego called his sister Luisa to tell her what had happened. At this stage the cops had no idea they'd just nicked a bunch of killers red-handed.

Later that same day, Little Egg's battered corpse was discovered but the police still didn't know they already had the guilty men locked up. It was only after some of the victim's family flew over for Little Egg's cremation service that the net started to close on La Patrona and her motley crew. Little Egg's Uncle Gersain gathered together some of his nephew's young London Colombian mates and urged them to take a long, hard look at their friend's battered and mutilated body as it lay in the morgue. 'I wanted to make them think what might happen to them if they didn't change their lifestyle,' Gersain later explained.

Meanwhile, killer cop The Skunk was openly bragging about his murderous habits back in Colombia where he'd killed several street children, burning them out of sewers where they lived. He also made it clear he'd plugged a young hoodlum in London as well.

Word soon reached Luisa's kid brother Diego that other Colombians were saying he played a part in the topping of Little Egg. After a couple more days young Diego spilled the beans to the Old Bill. They realised for the first time what a heavy duty case they'd stumbled upon.

Then the police SWAT team abseiled into Luisa's fancy gaff as she was leaving the premises in Royal Belgrave House to take her daughter to school. In the apartment they found £20,000 hidden in her knicker drawer. La Patrona also turned out to be a mobile phoneholic. She had eight different mobiles and was adept at answering three phones at the same time! Her phone records made very revealing reading. She was also outraged that anyone had dared to have the bottle to inform on her.

La Patrona's eventual trial at the Old Bailey's Number One court on 11 October 1999 lasted four months. In the witness box Luisa switched on the tear taps whenever she was accused of any deadly deeds. But it didn't cut much ice with the jury. And the judge told her and her hitmen, 'You all three have been convicted on compelling evidence of a cruel, cold-blooded contract killing. That youth was executed for no better reason than having the impertinence to steal a chain from Bolivar's lover's neck. You, Luisa, doubtless with Fernandez, who escaped to Spain shortly before the killing, hunted that young man down and were party to hiring two assasins to kill him in a most brutal and barbaric fashion. You showed him no mercy.'

A jury of six men and six women had deliberated over three days before reaching their unanimous guilty verdicts. The trial cost the taxpayer £2 million and Cedeno and Jaramillo were ordered to be deported. After being sentenced to life for Little Egg's murder, Luisa's lawyer said his client would appeal against her conviction.

Not surprisingly, Luisa's little bro Diego is currently in a protected witness programme living in fear that he'll be the next one to be garrotted. He currently resides in a secret address in the north of England, but the cops admit they still don't really know why he was mug enough or courageous enough to point the finger at the evil coke baroness and her hired killers.

La Patrona's 16-year-old daughter, Sandra, who now lives at her father's council flat on a South London estate, still insists to this day, 'My mother is innocent. I am not allowed to tell you the real story.'

But the murder of Little Egg – a lowly pickpocket from the slums of Bogota – may have persuaded Luisa's bosses back in Colombia that breaking into the lucrative UK cocaine market as a direct supplier of drugs rather than a wholesaler was not as easy as they thought.

The police are still anxious to speak to her lover, drugs boss Snake Hips/Scarface Fernandez, who's since disappeared into thin air.

CHAPTER 7

CHAPTER

7

KENNY NOYE

'I hope you all die of cancer.'

**KENNY NOYE TO THE JURY
AFTER HE WAS FOUND GUILTY
OF HANDLING THE BRINK'S-
MAT GOLD BULLION.**

In the underworld, certain names resonate for the sheer, stunning audacity of their crimes. They're admired by new and old gangsters, they have the bent cops in their pockets, and they live on the very edge. Meet Kenny Noye.

Kenny was – and still is – one of the most powerful and richest criminals in Britain. A genius of the underworld, handling the proceeds of huge drug deals and legendary blaggings have helped make him tens of millions of quid. He's got a string of gorgeous birds scattered around the globe and he's enjoyed a five-star lifestyle. He's also another member of that exclusive gentlemen gangsters' club, the Brink's-Mat team. It's a legendary job that links so many of the names mentioned in this book.

Yet for much of the last 25 years Kenny Noye's been in the slammer although, typically, being under lock and key hasn't stopped him from operating as a master criminal who's earned the respect of every gangster across the nation. Kenny Noye's emergence as a major player is part of recent criminal history. It's a fascinating insight into life after the Krays and the Richardsons.

Kenneth John Noye was born in Bexleyheath, Kent, on 24 May 1947. Without smog and the inner city's concrete jungles of housing developments, Bexleyheath was the new face of south east London. It had many of the area's appealing features, but few of its bad habits. And there were some traditional reminders of London life – an excellent range of boozers, chippies and pie and eel shops.

At first Kenny Noye's folks found it strange swapping their tiny terraced house in the docklands for one of the square bungalows that dominated streets such as Jenton Avenue, Bexleyheath, where the Noyes lived. Kenny's father, Jim, had become a fully-trained communications engineer while serving his country with the Navy during the Second World War. Before that he'd been a junior docker in Bermondsey.

Jim Noye went on to become a telecommunications expert at the GPO. Kenny's mum Edith was a strong, blunt-speaking lady who took her young son under her wing from an early age. She worked three nights a week as manageress of the nearby Crayford Dog Track. The Noyes were proud that they both worked. Supporting the family was all that mattered in those days. There was no question of scrounging off the state – the Noye family didn't do things that way. They looked after their own.

And young Kenny Noye certainly proved quite a handful. At just three years old he broke his nose falling out of a tree in a neighbour's garden while pinching apples. It left him with a hooter like a prize fighter. When Kenny was five, he went to the corner shop with his mum, slipped behind the counter when no one was looking, opened the cash till and helped himself. Little Kenny was only caught when his mum saw a ten bob note (50 pence) sticking out of the top of his wellington boots as they were walking out of the shop.

Schoolboy Kenny was a charming, troublesome kid. These days they'd call him hyperactive. 'He got away with a lot because he was very cheeky,' his cousin Michael Noye told me a few years back, 'but he couldn't keep out of trouble for a minute. A right handful.' Young Kenny was already boasting about what he'd do when he grew up. 'Earn lots of money,' he pledged to anyone who'd listen.

In the gritty dockland areas of south east London where Kenny's old man had grown up, petty thieves were still nicking tea chests off lorries and selling every commodity they could lay their hands on. Truck drivers were kidnapped and had their loads stolen, but no one was harmed. Everything was fair game in those days; fags, booze and clothing. Railway containers were raided at night and their contents would end up on local street markets the next day.

Crime was an escape hatch for the unemployed, many of whom were part-time villains anyway. Then, in the early Sixties, armed robbery became the most lucrative form of income. In south east London the status of blaggers (robbers) put them on a par with film stars in the local community.

Meanwhile, teenage Kenny Noye was starting his criminal career. At Bexleyheath Secondary Modern he leaned on other school kids for protection money. A brief spell at printer's college followed but that soon gave way to nicking motors and scooters and selling them on to other villains in south east London and Kent.

Then Kenny got hooked up in the lorry haulage business. Soon he was making a packet handling stolen gear and even copping a few bob off the Old Bill at the same time by letting them in on a few secrets in exchange for some inside info on his rivals. Kenny called it back scratching. You scratch mine, I'll scratch your's.

Kenny married his teenage sweetheart Brenda and soon had two sons, Brett and Kevin. They moved to the peace and quiet of a village called West Kingsdown, in the Kent countryside, but still within shotgun range of his old south east London haunts. That's when Kenny decided to branch out and began fronting up cash for some daring blaggings. It was a smart move as one old lag explained, 'Kenny soon found himself handling half a dozen jobs at a time. The money was rolling in.' The beauty of Kenny's criminal career was that he rarely got his own hands dirty. He'd simply put up the finance for a job and then leave it up to his team.

By the time Kenny had turned thirty he was driving a Roller, running a fleet of fancy women and even had time to become a Mason in a cheeky bid to get closer to the police, judges and politicians who were also members. The Freemasons were a strange mob. Many saw them as a secretive organisation, but others believed they were nothing more than a discreet gentlemen's club with tens of thousands of members across Britain. How much power and influence they wield through this country's politicians and lawmakers will probably never be known. But Kenny Noye knew that being a member would certainly be good for his type of 'business'.

As one cop later explained, 'Kenny Noye cynically manoeuvred himself into the Masons as if it was the right pub for him to be seen at.' Some police members of the West London Masons lodge which Kenny joined were outraged by the presence of such a villain in their 'club'. But others saw people like Kenny as an opportunity to pick up a good informant.

Secret police records relating to Kenny's criminal career up until this stage were supplied by a police source to this author in March 2000. They show just how active Kenny already was back in those early days.

On 10 October 1981, Kenny appeared in Canterbury Crown Court for importation of a firearm, evasion of VAT, providing a counterfeit document after his arrest, making a false statement to the VAT and breaking the conditions of an earlier suspended sentence. He was very lucky to get a suspended prison sentence plus a £2,500 fine. Many believe to this day that Noye's 'friends' in the police force helped him avoid a spell inside.

Then the cops put Kenny Noye under regular surveillance in a bid to trip him up. They even carried out a few raids with search warrants on his home in West Kingsdown. A Crime Intelligence Report stated that Kenny was running a stolen motor vehicle parts ring which also involved exporting lorry equipment to Syria. He was even rumoured to have supplied some of the heavy-lifting vehicles used to construct the Thames Barrier. Kenny had a finger in a hell of a lot of pies.

Ambitious Kenny was even rather partial to using the alias of Kenneth James when he wanted to travel incognito. He also kept a luxury flat in Broomfield Road, Bexleyheath, where neighbours spotted him in the company of some tasty-looking birds. The police soon linked Kenny to more than a dozen companies and his list of 'associates' read like a *Who's Who* of the south east London and Kent underworld. Besides his Roller, Kenny drove a Jeep and various Fords that he bought directly from Fords in Dagenham through a contact. Kenny sold them on for a fat profit.

One of Kenny's former employees at his lorry yard in West Kingsdown told the cops he was terrified of Kenny and stated that he had 'suffered violence at the hands of Noye in the past'. Even back in the early 1980s, the police reckoned Kenny was dabbling in the drug trade. One time they watched him pass over £10,000 in cash to an unnamed man in the Black Swan pub, on the Mile End Road. They had no doubt it was drug money. The same informant also told the cops that Kenny had handled the proceeds from a robbery in the Blackwall Tunnel.

The police report at the time stated, 'Noye allegedly puts up the money for organised crime, he is an associate of prominent London criminals. Noye travels to and from America and the Continent to allegedly change money.' He was certainly getting around.

The Old Bill reckoned Kenny had provided hundreds of thousands of stolen bricks for the construction of a housing estate. But when the secret police report named an MP with whom Kenny 'had a business association' it made Kenny look like an even more top-notch operator.

That report also featured Kenny's full criminal record to that time:

14.12.66 Old Street Magistrates Court. Found on enclosed premises for unlawful purposes. 12-month conditional discharge and £2.20 costs.

20.6.67 South East London Q.S. Receiving stolen vehicles. Receiving stolen property. Found on enclosed premises for unlawful purpose. Borstal Training.

20.5.75 Marlborough Street Magistrates Court. Theft of sunglasses. Assault on police. Fined £50. Ordered to pay £15 costs. Also fined £15.

21.2.77 Croydon Crown Court. Handling stolen property (five cases). Possessing document with intent to deceive. Unlawful possession of a shotgun. For all the charges Noye was fined £2,100 and ordered to pay almost £8,000 in compensation plus costs. He also got a two-year suspended prison sentence.

21.3.79 Malling Magistrates Court. Dishonestly abstracting electricity. Fined £250.

In 1982, Kenny proved he had a soft side by showing the hand of kindness to a neighbour in distress. The Noyes offered West

Kingsdown greengrocer Alan Cramer their sincere condolences when his 26-year-old son was killed in a car crash on nearby Death Hill. Mr Cramer was very touched by their concern: 'They sent me a nice letter with their condolences. It was one of the first we got. They said that if there was any help we needed we only had to ask and they would help in any way they could and they didn't mean moneywise. It was a nice thought.'

Many years later Mr Cramer returned the Noyes' offer of kindness by staunchly sticking up for Kenny when he faced some major headaches with the law.

As Kenny Noye's criminal enterprises continued to expand so did his 'back scratching' with a section of the police. He and a few other faces occasionally collected 'reward money' for pointing the cozzers in the right direction. This also enabled him to keep all his own illegal activities going unhindered.

Kenny's ascendancy coincided with a complete overhaul of the gangster's biggest enemy – the Met's Flying Squad. Instead of dealing with all serious crimes, the Sweeney were ordered only to tackle armed robberies. The squad's officers formed a central robbery squad run from a co-ordinating unit at Scotland Yard with four smaller groups dotted around London.

But it was the Brink's-Mat job which really put Kenny Noye on the map – and gave him respect throughout the London underworld.

* * *

The Brink's-Mat robbery is the stuff of legends. To nick so much gold and get away with enough to set dozens of people up financially for life was a gangster's dream come true.

But the sheer size of the Brink's-Mat haul of gold bullion created a major headache for the villains involved in the raid. The gang needed a mechanism, a conduit down which the gold could travel. It had to be smelted and sold into industry before any of the dosh could be shared amongst the BM team.

Some months after the blagging, a unit of undercover cops were ordered to hide out in the 20-acre garden of Kenny's vast home, Hollywood Cottage, in West Kingsdown, Kent, and see what he was up to. One night Kenny heard some movement in the bushes and charged right in and struck out at a black-clad figure he later claimed he thought was an intruder. Kenny used all his brute strength to smash his fists into the man over and over again. Then he pulled out a blade and began to plunge it into the body of undercover detective John Fordham.

In Hollywood Cottage, Brenda Noye rushed upstairs and grabbed a shotgun from one of at least half a dozen the couple kept in their bedroom cupboard. Loading the gun as she ran, Brenda Noye and Kenny's fellow Brink's-Mat operative Brian Reader headed down the drive in the direction of where they'd heard Kenny shouting. Kenny was standing over the masked figure, his Rottweilers growling.

'Who are you?' shouted Kenny angrily. 'Who are you?'

Detective Fordham was still wearing his balaclava hood.

Kenny noticed the officer's night-sight binoculars. He later claimed he thought he was dealing with a rapist or a peeping tom. Then Kenny knelt down and opened Fordham's jacket to get a closer look at the wounds he had inflicted a few moments earlier. In a much quieter voice he asked Fordham, 'What're you doing here?'

Fordham didn't answer because he was close to death. Moments later police swarmed into the grounds of Hollywood Cottage and arrested Kenny for murder.

Nearly a year later, Kenny was acquitted of murdering Detective Fordham, but the long arm of the law got its revenge when he was later banged up for nine years for his role in handling the gold bullion from the Brink's-Mat blagging that links so many of this country's big-time gangsters.

Make no mistake about it, the slammer was not the place for Kenny Noye or any major league gangster. Prison was there to take away his liberty, to lock him up and keep him from his beloved family and away from society. But Kenny knew the first man out of the gate was the cleverest man. He left the trouble-making to other, lesser mortals.

All around him in prison were drug addicts, homosexuals and social misfits. He saw it as a den of vice. He watched inmates inject themselves with filthy needles. He heard the gossip about who were the 'girl-boys' and who'd just give blow jobs. None of it mattered to him because he had businesses to run. He was above the riff-raff and everyone knew it.

As one former south east London thief taker later pointed out, 'Like other parts of life there's a pecking order in prisons, and the more successful the criminal is the higher up the pecking order he will be. He'll have an easier life because he'll have gofers running around doing his chores for him.'

In 1987 – during a spell inside the relatively easy-going Swaleside Prison on Kenny's manor of Kent – Kenny met a psycho-drug peddler called Pat Tate who told him all about a new designer drug called Ecstasy, which was just starting to take off in Britain. Pat Tate convinced Kenny to invest £30,000 in one of his Ecstasy deals. Many villains reckon that it was the first of millions of pounds of Brink's-Mat cash that helped flood Britain with Esctasy in the late 1980s and early 1990s.

(Tate, his partner Tony Tucker and another drug dealer called Craig Rolfe were later shot dead at point blank range as they sat in their Range Rover in an Essex field.)

Legend has it that Kenny made £200,000 back from that original £30,000 investment. Drugs were undoubtedly where the really big profits could be made. Blaggings would soon be a thing of the past. Like all good operators, Kenny Noye knew it was time to change direction. From inside nick, Noye invested vast sums of his considerable fortune, estimated in the late 1980s at £10 million, in the drugs explosion.

On his release from prison in 1994, Kenny decided to branch out into some high-tech villainry by joining forces with his old mate John 'Little Legs' Lloyd to form what later became known as 'The Hole-in-the-Wall Gang'. One of their members was a timid computer geek called Martin Grant who was recruited to help churn out plastic counterfeit credit cards which were then going to be used to withdraw money in one specific 24-hour period. Kenny reckoned the gang could net at least £100 million.

When Grant turned grass the police were so worried that Kenny and his team might get to him they put him in a safe house with armed cops on patrol day and night. He was only ever moved by helicopter. Grant later explained, 'Remember, I have seen the other side of Kenny Noye not so much against me but against others who have mucked him about. Although he can be a very nice chap he is quite capabale of turning into an aggressor.'

When the police finally moved in to arrest Kenny he was nowhere to be seen so they ended up nicking Little Legs and the rest of the Hole-in-the-Wall crew. Naturally, none of them were stupid enough to put the finger on Kenny. The law couldn't touch him even though they knew he was the main man behind the entire caper.

In May 1996, Kenny Noye made the biggest mistake of his life when he knifed to death motorist Stephen Cameron in a roadrage attack on the M25, just a few miles from his Kent home. Within hours of fleeing the scene, Noye was in a chopper rising above the countryside just outside Bristol to begin a two-and-a-half-year spell on the run from the police.

Back on the ground, Kenny's brand new Land Rover Discovery containing the knife he'd used to kill Stephen Cameron was being driven in a bizarre three-car convoy to Dartford, Kent, where it was scrapped by being crushed into a compressed box of jagged steel.

Kenny's role in the road-rage killing focused a lot of unwelcome attention on the south east London underworld. The police started wondering if Noye had been topped because other gangsters didn't like the extra heat they were suffering as the Old Bill frantically searched for the fugitive. Wherever Kenny Noye was in those early days after his escape, he was paying a heavy price for being linked to the Cameron killing.

As one former thief taker commented at the time, 'Kenny Noye may be a natural born criminal with a vast network of contacts, but will they keep him one step ahead of the police for ever?'

In the late summer of 1996, Kenny slipped quietly back into Britain and began moving from safe house to safe house. His impressive network of informants and contacts meant that he was safer here than in so-called unknown territory abroad. Such was his status in certain parts of Kent that he could drink and live relatively openly without the fear of being nicked. It was a measure of the power wielded by Kenny Noye.

Kenny was also taking a leaf out of his old friend John 'Little Legs' Lloyd's book. He'd done exactly the same thing when he was a supposed fugitive in America following the Brink's-Mat blagging. The nearest the cops ever really got to grabbing Kenny was in early 1997 when an anonymous tipster said that he was holed up in a small terraced house in Catford. They swooped on the house with armed officers but Kenny had long gone.

South east London criminal Gordon McFaul saw Noye in a pub in Dartford, Kent, in the spring of 1997. 'I wasn't surprised to see Kenny in the pub, he didn't have to hide. No one would grass him up,' explained McFaul. 'I had a drink with him. He seemed on good form. The bloke wasn't hiding from no one.'

Kenny was deliberately making sure he was seen out in some of his old haunts to let people on the manor know he'd done nothing wrong in his own eyes. He told anyone who would listen that he was innocent of the Cameron road-rage killing. 'But the cozzers will nail me for it anywhere. I don't stand a chance,' Kenny told one old south east London mate.

As another associate explained, 'It was important for Kenny to be seen out and about. He was tellin' his cronies that he wasn't scared of the Old Bill or no one. He was basically sayin' that if they wanted to find him they could come and try. But he had got the contacts and the knowledge to always be one step ahead of the game.'

Even Kenny Noye's cousin Michael – who'd joined him on many childhood exploits – was watched closely by the police as they desperately tried to discover where Noye had gone. 'They thought he'd get in contact with me but Kenny had more sense than to do that,' Michael Noye later told me.

In 1997, Kenny moved himself to an isolated village in southern Spain, but continued popping back and forth to south east London for important meetings despite being Britain's Public Enemy Number One. He even put up some dosh for a tasty plot to spring a drug baron from inside Whitemoor Prison, in Cambridgeshire. It involved smuggling in quantities of Semtex explosive, blasting a hole in the jail wall and then flying their man to freedom in a chopper.

One of the prison screws was nicked after an inmate leaked the escape plans to prison bosses. The man Kenny wanted to spring was an old pal serving an 18-year stretch inside Whitemoor for his part in a £65 million drug-smuggling operation. Kenny and a number of other gangsters had invested millions of pounds in this fellow's drug ring. 'Kenny needed to get the man out so they could recoup their orginal investment,' explained one source.

In November 1997, three of Noye's closest associates travelled by private plane to Spain's Costa del Sol to meet a gang of well-known drug dealers and armed robbers who agreed to acquire the Semtex and hire a helicopter. Kenny and his mates each threw in £100,000 to help finance the escape plan.

The gang had an informant who was working inside Whitemoor who'd agreed to smuggle the Semtex into the prison.

It was a classic Kenny Noye-backed operation; the screw had been trapped into helping the gang because he'd been caught having it off on the sly with some bird. That same screw was already supplying many inmates with drugs inside Whitemoor.

Prison authorities foiled the escape plan just a week before it was due to happen. Kenny was spitting blood because now he knew he wouldn't get back that lost investment of several million pounds.

And Kenny's own costs for staying on the run at his Spanish hideaway were proving sky high. He was shelling out £50,000 a month to keep one step ahead of the cops. 'He was greasing palms, paying for birds, his missus, you name it. And he was having to only deal in cash otherwise the cozzers might get wind of his movements,' explained one of his old Costa del Sol mates who saw him occasionally while he was on the run.

It can now be revealed for the first time that both the British and Spanish police had Kenny in their sights months before he was finally nabbed – but no one recognised him! And Kenny's life on the run didn't stop him from earning tens of millions of pounds in drug deals from his Spanish hideaway. He even boasted that he was still paying crooked cops back home to keep him one step ahead of the law.

My enquiries show that Kenny was so heavily involved in puff smuggling that he visited Yardies in Jamaica while he was on the run. He was even monitored by British police in Gibraltar with a local drug baron, but no one recognised him. Kenny travelled in and out of Gibraltar on a false UK passport without even having to show his photo ID and was photographed by the Spanish cozzers with a local girlfriend called Mina because she was under surveillance. But again, no one recognised him.

In Spain, Kenny bought a luxury yacht for £200,000 and chartered it out to drug smugglers. And he so terrified the owner of the house he'd bought in the tiny village of Atlanterra, that the man went into hiding in Germany after accepting Noye's cash no-questions-asked offer.

One time volatile Kenny even pulled a knife on a middle-aged neighbour in Atlanterra when the man climbed over Noye's gate to talk to his gardener. Frequently Kenny secretly smuggled his father, wife Brenda and other relatives and mates to his home in Spain even though the Old Bill in Kent were supposed to be shadowing their every move. And Kenny wasn't even spotted when twenty Spanish cops patrolled the next door house because one of Spain's senior politicians spent the summer at the property.

But even Kenny Noye can be taken to the cleaners occasionally; in Spain he was conned by a local so-called property developer into investing £100,000 into the renovation of a local hotel which never happened. Throughout his stay in Spain, Kenny flew various mistresses out to Portugal then smuggled them across the border and rented them isolated houses at least ten miles from his own home.

Yet he continued travelling extensively from his Spanish hideout. His false passport contained numerous stamps showing that he had been a regular visitor to Jamaica and Morocco. One Noye associate explained, 'Kenny was up to all sorts of deals. He went to the home of a British villain living in Morocco and they set up a smuggling operation together. Then he linked up with a West Indian he'd been inside Swaleside Prison with and they met some seriously heavy Yardies in Jamaica.'

In mid-June 1998, the police back in Kent had a lucky break when they got a call from a long-time informant who gave them the mobile phone number of another villain who was in regular contact with Kenny Noye. When the grass demanded a £100,000 tip-off fee if it led detectives to Noye, the cops started to take him very seriously.

Kent Plod immediately requested assistance from MI5, who sanctioned round-the-clock surveillance of the target's phone from their headquarters overlooking Vauxhall Bridge in London. MI5 – Britain's domestic security service – had some really tasty surveillance equipment and had been helping police across the country with their enquiries since the mid-1990s.

By the end of August 1998, Kenny had been traced to his house in the tiny Spanish seaside village of Atlanterra, just south of the city of Cadiz. Days later he was arrested in a nearby restaurant by Spanish and Kent cops and slung in a shithole jail in Cadiz. His gorgeous brunette girlfriend disappeared into thin air before the cops could find her.

Even while awaiting extradition from jail in Spain Kenny flirted with a tasty female prison officer in custody in Cadiz. Prison source Oscar Labato later explained, 'Noye was only in that prison a few days when a male officer noticed that he was spending increasing amounts of time talking to this particular woman officer. She was immediately transferred to another wing of the prison.' Just a couple of months later the same woman screw was fired for having sex with an ETA terrorist inmate. She was later reinstated after claiming unfair dismissal even though she admitted having an affair with an inmate. She has never revealed exactly what happened with Noye.

Kenny's team of highly paid Spanish briefs reckoned he stood a good chance of avoiding extradition. But in March 1999, a bunch of Madrid judges threw out all his appeals and Kenny knew he'd be heading home within a few weeks.

Back in Britain, the tabloids revealed that Kenny's missus Brenda was having a romance with a Cornish fisherman. Some cops reckoned the article had been deliberately fed to Fleet Street to make it clear Brenda Noye was no longer married to Kenny. One Kent police contact explained, 'It makes Noye look more like the victim rather than the perpertrator. It also makes Brenda a hostile witness. In other words, she can't testify against him.'

Finally, on 20 May 1999 – after a couple of last ditch appeals by Kenny's briefs had failed – Kenny was handcuffed and ordered out of his cell at Madrid's Valdemoro Jail. Then he was bundled into an anonymous white van escorted by two plain Seat saloons out towards the city suburbs. Less than thirty minutes later Noye was handed over to three Kent policemen at Madrid Airport and secretly flown to London's Gatwick Airport.

The following day, 21 May, Kenny appeared before magistrates in his old manor of Dartford to hear the murder charges concerning the death of Stephen Cameron. Kenny was immediately taken to the most secure prison in London – Belmarsh Jail – and placed in solitary confinement at his own request.

Back in England, the London underworld was buzzing with rumours about who'd grassed up Kenny Noye. Stories were circulating that the informant had qualified for £100,000 reward money … but would he live long enough to enjoy it? As one criminal source said at the time, 'I can tell you there'll be an even bigger price on that bastard's head for turnin' in Kenny Noye.'

Once in Belmarsh high-security jail, Kenny lorded it over his entire wing and greeted various south east London screws like they were long-lost old friends. One fellow Belmarsh inmate told me in a series of tape-recorded telephone interviews, 'Kenny Noye was the king inside here. He knew many of the staff and inmates already from when he previously served time. Some of them even knew him from his days as a petty villain in south east London and Kent. It was like home from home for him. The staff said he'd been given his own wing at Belmarsh for his own protection but his guys in the main part of the prison said that Kenny had requested to be isolated because he hoped he could secretly carry on running all his rackets without interruption.'

Kenny even got people inside Belmarsh to run errands for him and there were rumours that he had a mobile phone with him at all times. 'Noye had his own team of cronies in the main part of the prison,' explained my man in Belmarsh. 'It's all a game to Noye. Prison doesn't stop him operating. It's just an inconvenience.'

Kenny even let it be known that he was so confident he'd be aquitted of the murder of Stephen Cameron that he'd authorised his sidekick in Spain to get his house ready for his return. He even bunged thousands to his builder back in Spain from his prison cell. 'He was that confident he'd get off. His cronies were spreading the gospel according to Noye around the entire prison. It's a game that Noye is very good at,' added the inmate.

In November 1999, I was approached by a Kenny Noye contact and asked if I wanted to meet one of the money men who had known all about Kenny's movements while he'd been on the run. The meeting was to take place in a hotel bar to the west of London and, my contact warned me, 'This geezer will get up and walk away if you try and ask him anything directly about Kenny Noye.'

The man who showed up spent the following three hours telling me in great detail about most of Noye's movements during his two and a half years on the run. And when it came to explaining why many other criminals wanted to bring Noye's flight from justice to an end, this fellow said, 'It was time for the cozzers to haul Kenny in. He knew they'd catch up with him in the end.'

All the gossip and rumours surrounding the so-called roadrage killing of Stephen Cameron were finally put to rest when Kenny Noye walked into the number two court of the Old Bailey on Thursday, 30 March 2000 – nearly four years after that murder on the M25. Gone was the confident swagger that had accompanied Kenny's last appearance in the very same dock of the very same building 14 years earlier. This time Kenny, now grey-haired and dressed in a grey cardigan, sat hunched almost like an old man in the dock between three prison officers. His eyes panned the jury of eight women and four men from the moment he was led in by three prison screws.

Before the case could proceed, the judge Mr Justice Latham ordered round-the-clock protection for each juror. He even told them all, 'There are many people who have an interest in this case and its outcome. I have arranged for you to be provided with escorts that will, I am afraid, affect your daily life to some extent.'

Kenny claimed he was simply defending himself when he pulled a knife out from under the front seat of his car and stabbed Cameron to death on the M25 roundabout. But the jury didn't believe him and found him guilty of murder by a verict of 11-1.

Kenny let out a deep gasp and held his head in his hands when he heard the verdict. Victim Stephen Cameron's father leapt from his seat just feet away, hands aloft in celebration and shouted, 'Yes.'

Then Mr Justice Latham told Kenny, 'The jury having found you guilty of murder, there is only one sentence I can impose and that is one of life imprisonment.' Kenny looked unsteady on his feet as the three screws led him down the 21 steps from the dock of number two court to the cells below. A few minutes later a van, its siren blaring, took him back to Belmarsh.

Outside the court DS Dennis McGookin, the Kent officer who led the last two years of the road-rage investigation, said, 'He's an evil man. He's been jailed for life and that's where he should remain.'

After the verdict, the son of Kenny's earlier 'victim', DC John Fordham, broke his family's 15-year silence on Kenny. 'You make your own tomorrows and I think he has made his. You can't go on committing crimes,' said John Fordham. 'I am very pleased for the Cameron family, very pleased with the verdict. But it doesn't bring my dad back.'

In the hours following the verdict, it emerged that Kenny's defence, estimated to have cost between £500,000 and £1 million, had been funded by the taxpayer. He'd been granted legal aid because on paper he was not worth a penny.

Meanwhile, Kenny Noye's criminal status as Public Enemy Number One would ensure he received the utmost respect from staff and inmates at whatever prison he ended up in. As one policeman pointed out, 'This isn't the last we shall hear of Kenny Noye.'

And there's no doubt Kenny's crime empire will continue to expand, even from inside prison. South east London face Gordon McFaul reckons, 'Noye's addicted to crime. Nothing stops him. His reputation as a master criminal is second to none. If it wasn't for his filthy temper the rest of the world wouldn't even know who he was.'

In the late summer of 2000, Kenny even pocketed half a million quid from the sale of his luxurious Spanish home – and authorities couldn't touch a penny of it! Kenny got top dollar for the gaff by pouring £30,000 into improvements despite being in the slammer for the previous two years.

He even splashed out hundreds of pounds on getting special glossy sales brochures with photos circulated amongst his criminal associates in a bid to sell the house. 'Noye continues to operate even from a prison cell. It's outrageous,' said one of his neighbours in Spain, Hermann Ritz. 'He behaves more like a property developer than a convicted murderer.'

Kenny believes that despite a pledge from authorities to seize all his assets, they will be powerless to grab the proceeds from the house sale because, in legal terms, he never actually owned the property. It was never registered in his name.

'Kenny's been buying and selling property like this for years in other people's names,' explained one source in south east London. 'He used to do it to avoid paying taxes but it's come in even more handy now that everyone's after his dosh.'

Kenny even threw in his beloved £20,000 blue Shogun jeep for good measure. Added his associate, 'Kenny really thought he'd be acquitted over the M25 killing and would return here to live out the rest of his days, so when he got the life sentence the first thing he did was ensure the house was sold.'

Kenny Noye is supposed to be one of the Home Secretary's biggest targets in his bid to confiscate money and property from Britain's gangsters. But he still currently owns at least SIX properties around the world worth at least TWO MILLION POUNDS. 'Kenny's laughin' really. He knows that no one can touch those properties abroad and he's made sure that everythin' he's financed in Britain is in other people's names,' explained one underworld source. 'You could call it Kenny's pension policy. He reckons he'll be out of prison one day and he wants to make sure he doesn't have to struggle.'

Kenny still currently owns a share in a hotel in Spain, a timeshare holiday complex in Northern Cyprus, two penthouse apartments in a nearby town in Cyprus. His wife lives in a detached bungalow in Looe, Cornwall. His parents live in a recently built detached five-bed house on his old manor of West Kingsdown, Kent. Then there's the semi in Bexleyheath which he has in the past used to 'entertain' his mates.

In recent years, Kenny has also liquidated other assets including a fitness club in Dartford, Kent, sold for £150,000, the family home near Sevenoaks sold in 1998 for £500,000, an interest in a south east London winebar for £200,000 plus an interest in two boutiques in south east London sold for £300,000. Kenny is also believed to have retained part, if not whole, ownership of at least some of his former homes which were 'sold' for knockdown prices to criminal associates.

It's all a long way from the modest three-bed bungalow in Jenton Avenue, Bexleyheath, where Kenny was born and bred. Explained another of his criminal associates, 'Kenny Noye would have made a brilliant legitimate businessman but he couldn't resist the thrill of being a gangster.'

Kenny – the master manipulator – is currently locked up in top security Whitemoor Prison plotting his next move. Underworld sources initially believed that Kenny would name some top faces to the police in exchange for a reduced sentence. But then the key witness against him during the Cameron murder trial was gunned down by a hitman outside a shopping centre in Kent in the late summer of 2000. The murdered witness's wife told newspapers she did not believe her husband had told the truth during Kenny's Old Bailey trial. Shortly afterwards, Kenny's legal team announced they were putting together a serious appeal against his murder conviction.

But in October 2001 the high court quashed this appeal. Despite this 'setback', this certainly isn't the last we shall hear of Kenny Noye – Gangster Number One. He's already pledged to continue his appeal through the European Court of Human Rights. If there's a way out of doing his bird, Kenny Noye will find it.

CHAPTER
8

CHAPTER

8

RODDY McLEAN

'One of the coolest customers
I've ever encountered.'

EDINBURGH DETECTIVE.

R oddy McLean, big-time Scottish drug baron and alleged part-time police informant, is a man not to be crossed. A couple of years back one national tabloid featured him in its 'rich list' with a net worth of around £4.5 million. Roddy wasn't happy because he knew that sort of publicity could cause him a bucketload of heat.

But since then it's reckoned Roddy has more than doubled his fortune thanks to some shrewd property sales and an eye for the big deal that puts most of his rivals north of the border in the shade. Roddy, now 56, owns property worth more than £1 million plus land at Edinburgh's South Queensferry and a number of boats. So he was mighty relieved when he was forced to hand over just £100,000 compensation after a recent run-in with the law. It barely made a dent in his wallet.

At one time Roddy bought one of his drug smuggling boats from Customs for a cut-price deal. The *Sea Ranger V* offshore supply vessel and its multi-million pound cargo had been confiscated when its captain was arrested back in 1993. Months later Roddy paid £5,000 cash for the boat, even though it had a resale value of around half a million quid.

Later Customs officers claimed they'd given the boat to Roddy for a knockdown price because he was one of their most important informants – a claim that he has always strenuously denied. Anyway, Roddy immediately renamed the 150ft vessel the *Toto* before registering it in Belize and then transporting it from Leith in Scotland to a South African shipping agent for leasing. Many believe it was used many times to transport puff into Scotland.

Back on the mainland, the police eventually launched Operation Balvenie specifically to try and net Roddy. For almost a year they seemed to be getting nowhere fast. It was as if Roddy knew exactly what they were up to. Maybe he had 'a few friends on the force', so to speak. The cops dug into every aspect of Roddy McLean's lifestyle and he came up smelling of roses. He was shadowed everywhere he went. Ironically it was only when Roddy tried to give the Old Bill the slip that they stumbled on the fact he was setting up a huge drugs deal.

One day in May 1996, Roddy sauntered into Waverly Station in Edinburgh, cool as a cucumber, to catch a train to London. Customs officers were waiting for him and tailed him to a meeting with a fellow they later tagged as Brian Silverman, a link man with the Adams family, down in North London. Roddy was so obsessed with losing his shadows that he completely changed his travel plans on the journey back to Scotland. But the boys in blue had already spotted his link with Silverman.

Then a month later, Roddy was eyeballed by Customs investigators boarding another train from Edinburgh to King's Cross, in London. This time Customs officers managed to shoot some good-quality video camera footage of their subject talking to Silverman again. They knew something was about to go down.

On 11 June 1996, Customs men followed Roddy, his son Roderick Jnr and another associate as they travelled to

Milford Haven, Wales, where they purchased a former lifeboat called the *Ocean Jubilee*. Roddy handed over £29,000 cash for the vessel in a plastic carrier bag. Then he and the others sailed the boat back up to Scotland. On 20 June they arrived in Scrabster Harbour on the northern tip of the Scottish mainland, claiming the boat had developed gearbox problems. They moored the boat and scarpered in a car back to Edinburgh. That's when Customs officers decided to call in the cavalry in the shape of MI5 and their high-tech surveillance equipment.

Customs soon intercepted a mobile telephone call from a shop in Roddy's home town of Edinburgh to one of Spain's major puff operators, a fellow known only as Alf. That call convinced the Old Bill that Roddy and his merry men were about to pull off one of the deals of the century.

The spooks at MI5 then firmed up that Alf had used the same phone to call another number in Holland, which turned out to be the home of a well-known puff smuggler. That link between the shopkeeper and Roddy didn't do the flashy Scottish gangster any favours at all.

Another flurry of calls between Roddy and Alf in Spain followed. Then Roddy called his man in Holland and announced the puff deal was green for go. What Roddy didn't realise was that the flying Dutchman's boat – called the *Issolda* – was about to be tracked by two spy planes packed with state-of-the-art surveillance equipment.

On the evening of 26 July, Roddy sailed off in the *Ocean Jubilee* to a spot 90 miles off the Caithness coast. The *Issolda* soon showed up bobbing on the horizon. Roddy spoke to his Dutch counterpart using the codename Popeye. At 3:24am that morning the operation to hand over the three tons of puff began. Just as the loading had finished and the boats were drifting apart, Customs cutters moved in to intercept and board both vessels. The game was up. Sadly, during the operation, Customs officer Alastair Souter died when he was crushed between Roddy's boat and a Customs vessel.

Roddy was nicked for masterminding an attempt to smuggle three tons of puff into Scotland. One of his houses was swiftly sold shortly after his arrest while his wife Susan continued living in the family's other mansion in nearby Boswall Road. Yet, as if to prove to the world he was just a hapless villain, filthy rich Roddy McLean was given legal aid to fight the impending court case. Roddy claimed he had no other way of paying for his legal bills.

When the case finally got to the High Court in Edinburgh, fifteen armed coppers with drawn semi-automatic rifles surrounded the High Court and Parliament Square in the Scottish capital while Roddy and his mates stood trial. In court, Roddy Snr admitted smuggling the three tons of puff from Morocco while everyone else denied the charges. The trial was told how Customs men pounced on Roddy's boat the *Ocean Jubilee* just after the shipment of puff had been handed over on the high seas from that Dutch yacht.

But Roddy's brief Neil Murray QC claimed in court that his client was in serious debt through his shipping business and had got involved in the drugs operation to clear those debts. 'There is no doubt in my mind that the death of Mr Souter weighs very heavily on his conscience,' said the QC, referring to the death of the Customs officer.

But the judge Lord Dawson told the court, 'The volumes involved were truly in the major league; some £3 million would have been required to purchase such a vast consignment. The profits to be made were astronomical; the retail value of these drugs being estimated at more than £10 million.'

Roddy's mate Brian Silverman's links to the Adams family back in London were disclosed in open court, even though Silverman insisted he was not a major player in the drug smuggling operation. After Silverman had given evidence, Lord Dawson told him, 'You attempted to play the part of a likeable East End rogue in order to try and hoodwink what you obviously regarded as a susceptible provincial jury. You were clearly in charge of the London side of operations and a major character in the plot.' As he was sentenced to 14 years, Silverman tried to shout down the judge. He screamed, 'I think Judge Jeffries, the hanging judge, would have been proud of you 200 years ago. This trial is going to come back and haunt you.'

Then Lord Dawson had a poke at Roddy, 'You put this deadly plan into operation, endangering the lives of a number of officers bravely doing their duty and caused the death of one such officer.'

Roddy was upset, but not that surprised, when he copped a heavyweight 28-year sentence. Seven others, including Roddy's kid, Roddy Jnr, were sent to jail for 12 years for their part in the smuggling operation. Roddy McLean and his associates have always believed they were hammered by the judge in the trial because of the 'accidental' death of Customs officer Alastair Souter. Roddy's son blew a kiss to the public gallery as he was sentenced and he raised his fist and shouted 'freedom' to the amusement of a dozen spectators.

Then the Old Bill really put the boot in by claiming Roddy had been so helpful to them that they'd turned a blind eye to many of his 'other activities' in Edinburgh. Labelling him a grass was as good as sentencing him to death. Others were quick to rush to Roddy's defence. One former associate insisted, 'That's a load of old bollocks. The coppers are just pissed off because neither Roddy nor his kid would grass anyone up. Do you think they would have got such heavy sentences if they'd been informing? Come off it!'

After sentencing, Roddy conveniently found himself sharing a cell with his son Roddy. Inside jail, screws uncovered a plot to kill the McLeans and made a point of letting the local press know they were 'taking the threats very seriously'. There was talk of a £7,500 payment being made to a hitman to plug Roddy Snr and another £5,000 to have his kid topped. Roddy later claimed the stories were put about by the police in order to pile pressure on the McLean family.

Prison staff privately admitted they thought the sentencing on McLean was 'pretty over the top considering he was only importing cannabis which half the staff and inmates in here like to smoke'.

In May 1999, Roddy McLean and his other major partner in crime had their jail sentences cut by seven years from 28 to 21 after lawyers acting for him accused his original trial judge, Lord Dawson, of adding to their sentence because of that Customs officer's death, even though nobody was found culpable of his homicide. A further two years was cut from McLean's sentence because he also happened to be a first time offender.

CHAPTER 9

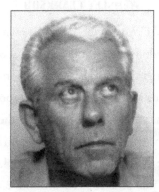

LITTLE LEGS

'I know he holds a grudge against
me and I'm very nervous about it.'

ONE-TIME ASSOCIATE
MARTIN GRANT.

John 'Little Legs' Lloyd is a legend in his own lifetime. And his fame in the London underworld doesn't just come from having been one of the original six Brink's-Mat bullion robbers who was never brought to justice. 'This guy is deeply respected everywhere,' says one old south east London blagger. 'He's the tops.'

Little Legs, now 61, is especially revered on his old manor of the East End where he grew up. He helped plan and carry out the Brink's-Mat job and copped around £5 million in the process. The Old Bill knew only too well that Little Legs and Kenny Noye went back a long way. Kenny even flogged him one of his old houses in West Kingsdown, Kent, which Legs' partner still lives in to this day. However, shortly after his old mate Kenny was nicked for handling the gold from the Brink's-Mat bullion raid, Little Legs sensibly did a runner.

The police told everyone he'd scarpered to America. In fact, Little Legs was popping back and forth to his old London and Kent haunts completely unbothered by the so-called worldwide manhunt in his name. He even boasted to one associate that he preferred flying back to London British Airways, 'Cos they've got a better safety record than all the other airlines.'

In the US, a Miami court ordered Legs in his absence to pay $400 million to Brink's-Mat insurers but he never coughed up a penny in Florida. Little Legs later described the court's decision as 'a fuckin' joke'.

As London's gangsters know only too well, Little Legs – nicknamed because of his spindly legs – has been a prime mover in many of the best-known blaggings of the last 30 years. His personal fortune probably tops the £10 million mark thanks to some shrewd investments of dirty money in a number of legitimate interests, including a transport business. At one stage, Legs also owned a car hire business in Kent. He was also a regular visitor to Clarke's Peacock Gym, in Canning Town, as well as often dropping in to his beloved Lovatt pub in the East End, for a swift pint.

While 'on the run' in the US, Little Legs even had his shorts specially tailored so they flattered his funny old pins. He also splashed out a few thousand bucks on some surgery to correct his disfigured toes. Back in London, a warrant was also issued for Legs' arrest in connection with Brink's-Mat and a £10,000 reward was offered. Legs' beloved common-law wife Jean Savage even copped a five-year sentence for conspiracy in connection with the Brink's-Mat raid. But more about the loyal and wonderful Jean later …

Then, in 1994, Little Legs was named on the *America's Most Wanted* TV crime show. A couple of weeks later Legs took the biggest gamble of his life by walking into Rochester Row police station with his brief to give himself up. The Crown Prosecution Service eventually ruled that there was insufficient evidence linking him to the Brink's-Mat job. The gamble had paid off.

Less than a year later, Legs reluctantly donated a five-figure sum to a consortium of insurance companies after he was fingered for his role in the 1983 Brink's-Mat bullion robbery even though there wasn't enough evidence to prosecute him in a court of law.

But gangsters like Little Legs Lloyd can't stay out of trouble for long. Soon he'd hooked up with some of his old Brink's-Mat mates for a caper they believed would top any other crime ever committed in Britain before.

At a pub just off the Old Kent Road, a small and dirty enough place to keep most ordinary punters out, and therefore chosen for its privacy by a number of south east London faces, Legs met up with Kenny Noye and some other familiar faces. Lloyd told his mates he was planning a cash card cloning scheme he believed could net them as much as £100 million.

Cash dispensers were the key to this daring crime and Lloyd needed some backers to come in with him. Kenny Noye immediately volunteered for a piece of the action for what was to become known as 'The Hole-in-the-Wall job'(also known as the ATM scam).

Noye and Lloyd put up some hefty finance to support the team of villains who would be spending months planning the crime. Then they used their own contacts in the nick to scout around for some technical recruits to the team. The idea was to tap into the latest banking technology and an army of corrupt communications engineers and computer experts had to be recruited to make vast numbers of cloned cashpoint cards. These would then be used to empty cash from the bank accounts of thousands of ordinary people. If they pulled it off it would throw the British banking system into total chaos.

Eventually, computer boffin Martin Grant was hired from inside Blantyre House open prison in Kent. He'd been jailed for attempting to murder his wife and child but in the slammer he'd studied for a degree in electronic communications. Grant was out on day-release for work experience at a van hire business owned by Paul Kidd, another villain involved in the cashcard cloning scheme with Little Legs.

Legs and his Hole-in-the-Wall gang planned to enter British Telecom exchanges with their team of corrupt engineers to put telephone taps on the lines and memory boards. The info would then be transferred to the gang's computer. But unknown to the gang, computer nerd Martin Grant, completely out of his depth with this team of pros, was already feeding information about the credit card scam to the law. He'd confessed to a prison chaplain about the planned robbery and later made a statement of over 300 pages to the Old Bill.

Later Grant provided a fascinating insight into Little Legs Lloyd and his mate Kenny Noye. 'Noye and Lloyd were just names to me at first. They meant nothing. But people inside prison talked about them as if they were gods.' Grant said he attended one meeting with the gang where Kenny and Legs produced prison paperwork on his (Grant's) record and family background which clearly had been given to Legs by prison staff. Those details included the addresses of Grant's mother and brother.

Then, in a chilling incident, Little Legs drove Grant up to his mother's house in the Midlands and walked him through the front door and even introduced himself to Grant's mother 'just to let me know he knew where she lived'. Grant later explained, 'John Lloyd then phoned Kenny Noye to say he had met my mum. I was so scared.'

Grant added, 'Kenny Noye and Lloyd told stories about hijacking vehicles in the early days and what they did to people who crossed them.' Grant said they also made continual references to other criminal associates in Spain and the United States.

Grant says that Kenny Noye and Little Legs became very threatening towards him once they began suspecting he might be grassing them up. 'One time they got a bunch of other villains to follow me back to prison to make sure I wasn't in touch with the police,' he said. Grant also recalled an incident when Noye and Lloyd almost came to blows after they had a problem with the computers they were using as part of the scam. 'I saw Noye lose his temper with Lloyd and it wasn't a pleasant sight,' is all he'll say to this day.

After the arrest of the Hole-in-the-Wall suspects, Martin Grant was put into police custody away from prison for his own protection. Detectives were so worried that Kenny Noye and Little Legs might harm Grant they put him in a safe house with armed officers 24 hours a day and only moved him by helicopter.

Grant is still worried about Little Legs to this day: 'I know he holds a grudge against me and I'm very nervous about it.'

After Little Legs copped a five-year stretch for his part in the Hole-in-the-Wall scam, I paid his lady Jean Savage a visit at their immaculate bungalow in West Kingsdown, Kent. It just so happens that they'd bought it off Kenny Noye more than a dozen years back. Jean was a charming woman, but her Rottweilers and seven-foot-high brick wall complete with electronically controlled gates were not so welcoming.

After a ten-minute chat on her CCTV I realised she wasn't going to let me in for a chat about Little Legs and his antics. In 1999, Legs was released from prison and nothing has been heard from him since.

'But he's around and he's looking for new business opportunities – or so I've heard,' one old south east London face told me recently.

CHAPTER 10

GOLDFINGER

'He's a serious, organised criminal.'

**RETIRED SCOTLAND YARD
DETECTIVE ROY RAMM.**

The long arm of the law finally caught up with John 'Goldfinger' Palmer at the Old Bailey in May 2001, when he copped an eight-year stretch. Over more than thirty years he's earned literally hundreds of millions of pounds from his role as the most shadowy so-called businessman in Britain.

Palmer became this nation's wealthiest prison inmate when he was jailed for operating the world's largest timeshare fraud. But that prosecution barely scraped the surface of his criminal enterprises which elevated him to the position of 105th wealthiest person in Britain, according to one published 'league table' in 2000. His nickname 'Goldfinger' came from when he was accused, and found not guilty, of handling the bullion from, yes you've guessed it, the Brink's-Mat robbery near Heathrow Airport in 1983.

The 51-year-old villain looked stunned as the Old Bailey jury delivered its guilty verdict after nearly six weeks of deliberation. You see, John Palmer considered himself to be untouchable and he so nearly got away with all of it.

In the dock that day, tough guy Palmer went a whiter shade of pale and was close to tears as he slowly took off his £10,000 Cartier wristwatch and handed it to his brief before being led away to the cells. Before disappearing, Palmer glanced across at Christina Ketley, his business partner and mother of their ten-year-old son. She was also convicted of involvement in the same fraud. (He's also got a wife and two daughters in the West Country.) Ketley, 37, was given a suspended sentence. The jury later threw out charges against Palmer's nephew, Andrew Palmer, aged 37.

Earlier in the proceedings, John Palmer even conceded to the court, 'I acknowledge I have a strong, dominant personality, probably from my background. I have always relied on my wits for the benefit of those near and dear to me.'

Over the previous eight months, the Old Bailey had heard evidence from several of the almost 20,000 mainly British couples who had been duped out of their life savings by Palmer's outrageous timeshare antics in Tenerife. It's reckoned his victims lost more than £30 million. The investigation into Palmer's activities and the eight-month trial (plus an earlier abandoned hearing) cost at least £15 million of public money.

Yet Palmer had been so supremely confident of once again escaping conviction he even defended himself in court. He was described by prosecutor David Farrer, QC, as 'the largest shark in the timeshare water'. He treated his victims like 'a bunch of mugs'. They ranged across the social spectrum from barristers to pensioners, with the elderly forming the bulk of his long line of 'mugs.'

A procession of senior police officers gave damning evidence against Palmer. Detective Roy Ramm, a former commander at Scotland Yard heavily involved with the prosecution of the Brink's-Mat gang, denounced him as 'a serious organised criminal'. But John Palmer wouldn't stand for that kind of allegation; he immediately accused Ramm and many of his colleagues of corruption.

Palmer and Ramm then glowered at each other as Ramm told the court how Palmer had been taped by TV reporters on *The Cook Programme* offering to launder £60 million worth of drugs money. A furious Palmer hit back by insisting that Ramm and his colleagues illegally lined their pockets with reward money from the loss adjusters involved in tracking down the Brink's-Mat gold. Each time Palmer accused Ramm of corruption, the ex-detective threw back at him the drug money allegations.

Palmer even suggested that the taxpayers could have been spared the expense of a costly trial if authorities had instead sued him. He proudly mentioned that he could easily have afforded a £50 million loss in that department.

'You don't know how rich I am,' he sneered at Roy Ramm. 'Were you aware of my private plane, and my two helicopters?' he asked, pausing for the Old Bailey jury to savour his performance.

John Palmer is mighty proud of his 'achievements'; he employs 3,000 people to run his timeshare empire. There are also the three pilots for his Lear jet which remained constantly on standby at an airport on the outskirts of London throughout his trial. There's also a six-man crew for his £6 million yacht, *Brave Goose of Essex*, plus the liveried chauffeur who drove him to court each morning. Not to mention gourmet cooks, butlers, landscape gardeners and numerous others at his various properties across the world. They include a converted coach house at Battlefields, near Bath, a huge villa in Tenerife complete with a pool stocked with rare albino frogs and a château in Caen, France, with two golf courses.

No wonder John Palmer is reputed to spend more than £1 million a year on a team of crack bodyguards, including a number of former SAS soldiers. 'This is a villain with enemies on both sides of the fence,' says one south east London criminal, who's had dealings with Palmer in the past.

Palmer's timeshare developments include the Royal Gardens and Flamingo Park in Tenerife. He also owns Harleys nightclub in nearby Playa del las Americas plus other hotels, amusement arcades and bowling alleys – all of them perfectly respectable places.

'Not bad for a scrap metal seller,' he proudly told the jury during his latest trial.

Palmer's original hearing on the same timeshare charges began in September 1999 but was abandoned after eight months because he successfully argued that adverse press publicity connecting him to his mate Kenny Noye had prevented him from getting a fair trial.

The retrial kicked off on 2 October 2000. Palmer opened his case by declaring to the jury, 'I have been portrayed as a gangster. I am not a gangster nor ever have been a gangster.'

During the trial, Judge Gerald Gordon had to intervene several times after Palmer began shouting and finger jabbing at police witnesses. While Palmer admitted to the jury that a fraud had taken place he insisted it had all gone on behind his back.

Palmer also claimed that his lover, Ketley, was innocent of any involvement. The jury then heard how Palmer had doubled her salary after they became lovers. He even appointed her head of one of his companies, Island Financial Services. Prime operator Palmer was so confident of walking free from the Old Bailey that he proudly showed prosecutors brochures of a £10 million leisure complex and a £40 million hotel that were still under construction in Tenerife.

Ironically, it's reckoned that much of his so-called business empire will survive his incarceration as he has a team of trusted lieutenants running it. An army of lawyers and accountants helped offset most of his companies so that little of his fortune could be touched while he was in jail.

Just like Kenny Noye, he will no doubt thrive despite being behind bars. 'It's a major inconvenience but he'll hardly go broke as a result of this prosecution,' says one of his oldest associates. Rumours that Palmer already has a prime job in prison that gives him virtually unhindered use of a private phone have been strongly denied by jail authorities.

Until his conviction at the Old Bailey, John Palmer had bathed in the glory of a long criminal career that helped make him one of the richest, most feared, yet secretive gangsters in Britain over the past thirty years.

One of seven children, he grew up in dismal poverty in

Birmingham where he swindled mates and associates out of cash when they all worked together in market stalls in the suburb of Solihull. Palmer bristled with pride whenever he told how, despite being a dyslexic who left school at 15, he had made it to the top. Some of his pals from the old days say he never completely learned how to read and write. After leaving school, Palmer joined his brother in a roof-tiling business, then went on to become a door-to-door salesman offering paraffin at knockdown prices.

One of his earliest clashes with the police was in 1973 when he was fined for handling a stolen motor. A spell dabbling in second-hand cars soon followed. Then, in 1976, he moved into a highly lucrative coin-dealing venture based in posh Mount Street, Mayfair. A switch into the furniture business led to a serious clash with the law at Bristol Crown Court in 1980 when he received two suspended six-month jail sentences for fraud. Palmer then moved into the jewellery trade in the West Country.

But he first came to the attention of Britain's premier team of thief-takers – the Flying Squad – when he was thought to be helping the Brink's-Mat gang melt down their gold bullion. Many police and villains alleged that Palmer kept some of the gold for himself and used the cash proceeds to go into the timeshare business in southern Spain.

When Spanish authorities got to hear about his alleged involvement in handling the proceeds of Brink's-Mat and a number of other high-profile crimes, he was invited to leave Spain, so he did a moonlight flit to Rio de Janeiro. Palmer then went and surprised his criminal associates and the police by volunteering to return to Britain to face trial for handling the Brink's-Mat gold. 'He was supremely confident that he would be acquitted,' recalls one old criminal associate. 'Some of us reckoned he had some kind of "arrangement" with someone. But no one had ever been able to really put the finger on him.'

In 1987, Palmer found himself at the Old Bailey charged with conspiring with Kenny Noye and his associate Brian Reader to dishonestly handle that Brink's-Mat gold. So many villains were lining up to take a pop at Palmer by this time that he wore body armour throughout the trial.

But Palmer's supreme self-confidence proved entirely justified when, after all the evidence was heard, the jury believed he was innocent and he walked free from the court. Typically, Palmer couldn't resist blowing a contemptuous kiss to detectives.

John Palmer insisted from that moment on that the police began a vendetta against him. His claims sounded mighty familiar to those of his old mate Kenny Noye, who always said the cops were out to get him. Rumours that Palmer was an informant who had swapped certain information with detectives to keep them off his back were fiercely denied by all and sundry.

'They have done anything to try and get me, and have spent millions and millions of pounds of public money to get me. I am not guilty,' he yelled after the Brink's-Mat trial.

Palmer then quickly set up a string of 13 timeshare resorts in Tenerife, in the Canary Islands, where tens of thousands of tourists would eventually be swindled out of their savings. Vast numbers of innocent punters were systematically tricked into buying timeshare apartments in Tenerife. They handed over large sums of money, which in many cases turned out to be their life savings after falling victim to lies and false promises made to them in a slick, well-orchestrated and thoroughly dishonest sales operation. They included retired police officers, war heroes and even a former trading standards officer.

In 1991, John Palmer turned up in court yet again; this time he copped an 18-month jail sentence – suspended for two years – after admitting an £85,000 swindle using false names to obtain mortgages.

Meanwhile, Palmer continued expanding his timeshare resort and his companies targeted existing timeshare owners through a rent/sell racket, or sold holidaymakers timeshares with the promise of the vast profits they could earn from letting them. The promise of a definite resell of the properties was the inducement to the punters to buy into Palmer's operation. His salesmen approached tourists with scratch-cards and told them they had won fantastic prizes, such as watches or trips to Disneyland. They were then asked to pick up the prizes from a luxury resort and when they arrived they were given a guided tour.

Palmer's sales staff then offered to sell tourists' existing timeshare apartments if they bought a new one at the resort ... but the original timeshares were never sold, leaving the victims heavily in debt.

Seduced by the Palmer-approved sales patter, those victims paid a deposit by credit card before being confronted with complicated and deliberately misleading paperwork. They were told their other timeshares would be sold within weeks but were urged to take out a loan to buy one of the new apartments, just in case.

Palmer's salesmen then advised them to contact certain finance companies to get the loan and particular resale companies to handle the sale of their old timeshares. But when their old apartments failed to sell and they tried to cancel their contracts they were unable to recover their money and lost thousands of pounds.

And even if the victims did not have a timeshare to trade, Palmer's army got them to buy one and told them that the rental they would charge over the first few years would pay for the purchase.

The irony of all this is that Palmer believed that by pouring all his ill-gotten gains into a (sort of) legit business like timeshare he would be able to live like a king and avoid the problems associated with his earlier criminal enterprises.

'The problem was that John Palmer couldn't run his business like a normal, honest person,' says one retired detective. 'He couldn't resist going for the maximum con, putting pressure on innocent people. Palmer believed the world was full of mugs and he was going to con the lot of them. And he very nearly got away with it ...'

CHAPTER
11

PAUL FERRIS

'I've always used a weapon of sorts - whether it be a baseball bat or knife.'

PAUL FERRIS 1994.

Paul Ferris is feared and respected on the mean streets of Glasgow; one of the wealthiest gangsters in the city's history. And that's quite an achievement when you consider that this Scottish city has been steeped in crime for more than a century.

Back in 1991, hardman Paul Ferris found himself up on charges of murder, kneecapping and drug dealing. He was accused of rubbing out big-time Glasgow drugs dealer Arthur Thompson outside his home in the city. At the time, Thompson, then 31, was serving an 11-year sentence for heroin dealing and was home on a three-day leave from prison.

The court case later starring Paul Ferris featured testimony from a bunch of Glasgow gangsters, all contradicting themselves about Paul's alleged role as one of Scotland's most notorious faces. Paul, then just 28, smiled broadly as the jury read out their 'not guilty' verdict. It was almost as if he knew he'd walk out of there a free man.

No doubt the jury noticed his 'chib', a scar from a knife slash, which runs from the right side of his mouth and curves down below his jawline. The Ferris hearing had been the longest murder trial in Scottish history, costing almost £1 million. Paul and his family come from Blackhill, a council estate in the north east of Glasgow. Everyone on the manor knew the Ferrises and the Thompsons had been waging a deadly turf war for years before Paul ended up in the dock.

Paul Ferris started in the game at a very young age. Bullied as a kid at school in the Glasgow tenements, by the time he was thirteen he'd been sucked into a life of violence in order to escape that childhood aggro. Paul later admitted that hitting back was the best way he could gain respect from his fellow teenagers. 'It also helped me protect myself from serious harm.'

To this day, Paul Ferris always carries a weapon. As he says, casually, with a shrug of the shoulders, 'I've always used a weapon of sorts – whether it be a baseball bat or knife.' Yet it could have all been so different for Paul. He'd been virtually adopted by Arthur Thompson Snr, who befriended the then teenager after he copped a firearms conviction before turning sixteen. Old man Thompson took Paul on as a debt collector, or 'enforcer' as they're known in the trade.

Thompson Snr has never said what he thinks about the fact Paul Ferris was the prime suspect in the later contract killing of his son. But from the moment he was cleared of the Thompson charges Paul Ferris was closely monitored by the police who were convinced a hitman would one day execute him.

Paul's gained a lot of respect down the years by always refusing to cough up to the full extent of his involvement in organised crime in Glasgow. But he did once admit, 'That doesn't mean you've to let people stand on your toes. For if they do that, you have got to jump on their neck and break it.' But Paul sticks to brief public statements that guarantee the legend of Paul Ferris continues to grow. It's crystal clear that Paul Ferris's violent habits – he has a tendency to get involved in aggro at the drop of a hat – coupled with his level head, quick mind and easy charm make him one of the most influential gangsters of the Nineties.

But Paul plays it all down. He doesn't even look much like a hardman. He's not physically intimidating. He looks more like a tame businessman in his suit with his mobile phone ringing constantly. He smiles a lot and talks with a quiet tone that hardly ever goes beyond a whisper. 'But you cross him at your peril,' says one who should know.

Just ask the cops in Manchester. He was acquitted of possessing crack cocaine in Lancashire after convincing a jury in the city that he was taking the highly addictive drug to improve his skin. 'How he got away with that I'll never know,' says one thief taker bitterly.

Not surprisingly, Paul is constantly looking over his shoulder. When he was pulled up on the M4 one time after being chased at 130mph by cops in an unmarked Merc he claimed he thought it was full of hitmen. 'There have been events in the past where guns have been fired from strange vehicles,' he later explained. Once again no charges were preferred against the renowned gangster.

Many in Glasgow believe that Paul Ferris's fury with the Thompson family was sparked by the violence inflicted on his own father Willie Ferris. In the 18 months before Paul went for trial on those charges of murdering Arthur Thompson Jnr,

Paul's dad was beaten about the head with a hammer and baseball bat, knocked to the ground and slashed with a razor. After one attack he needed 100 stitches.

Meanwhile, Paul's elder brother, Billy, a convicted murderer who was given permission to move to a jail closer to his disabled father, continues to insist, 'I'm the only killer in the Ferris family.'

And throughout all this, Paul Ferris was alleged to be involved in a drugs operation which was netting at least £20,000 a week supplying virtually all the heroin in Glasgow – a city of 900,000 where there are 12,500 injecting drug addicts.

In the Nineties, as the legend of Paul Ferris grew and grew, so did the number of his encounters with local law enforcement. Inevitably, the man other villains jealously call 'Houdini' eventually found himself boxed into a corner.

Paul landed in hot water after a bizarre incident hundreds of miles from Glasgow when police in Lancashire boarded a night train on which a rowdy Scotsman was drinking heavily and annoying other passengers. He turned out to be armed with a .22 pistol, a silencer and 60 rounds – standard kit for a hitman.

The next day, while this would-be shootist was being held by the Old Bill, a number of frantic calls were received on his mobile phone and pager. Those calls linked him to Paul Ferris and a bunch of other Glasgow hoods. The cops then put the thumbscrews on their drunken hitman. They knew this was a chance to nick Houdini – Paul Ferris.

Undercover police mounted an operation to shadow Paul and his suspected arms dealing ring. They watched as Paul helped load three machine guns, silencers, four detonators and a box of ammo into a car after paying out £4,700 to a gun dealer right slap bang in the middle of the Adams Family's manor in Islington, North London. Amongst the weapons were special blue-tipped bullets which travel below the speed of sound so there's less of a bang when they're fired. The cops rapidly concluded Paul was a member of an arms gang on a run from Glasgow to London. They moved in and nicked the lot of them.

Paul and three others eventually found themselves at the Old Bailey where they all denied conspiracy to sell or transfer prohibited weapons and conspiracy to deal in firearms with three others. They also denied possession of explosives. Paul defended himself in court by claiming he thought the box in which the weapons were found contained material for a fraud he was involved in. He told the court he had no idea there were weapons in the box. The court heard how Paul Ferris was spotted putting all the armoury in a green Nissan Prairie, destination unknown. The Old Bill even found the £4,700 in Scottish banknotes in a jiffy bag that had Paul's fingerprints on it.

Paul, who at the time gave his address as Hogganfield Street, Glasgow, was eventually jailed for ten years for his part in the gun-running operation. It turned out all the weapons were on their way to gangs of villains in Manchester, Liverpool and Glasgow, for whom Ferris had become the main supplier. Judge Henry Blacksell told Paul Ferris after convicting him, 'One hardly dares speculate the potential death and destruction that may have been caused if they had reached their intended destination.'

Serving his sentence for gun-running, Paul found himself locked up and bored in Frankland Jail, Durham, so he decided to pen his life story in a book. Paul, who freely admitted delivering some serious stabbings to rivals and beating up others, insisted in the book he was harrassed and framed by the police and two of Scotland's most powerful gangsters.

Like so many of the other faces featured in this book, this is by no means the last we will hear of Paul Ferris, who was released from prison in 1999.

CHAPTER
12

THE HOLLOW HIPPY

'We know he's one of the richest villains in Britain.'

ONE OF THE COPS WHO NICKED HIM.

The boys in blue reckon drugs baron Andrew Billimore has made a whopping £600 million as a premier league dealer over the past 20 years. Even if he's only made a tenth of that he's worth a place in this book. Andy's network is so vast that at one point the Old Bill claimed he was boasting of importing coke worth up to £2 million a week.

Yet the 35-year-old former Cathedral guide (I kid thee not) has officially been 'unemployed' throughout this period. But then Andy Billimore is a master at keeping things low key. No flash motors, luxury mansions or fancy women for Andy.

He's studiously avoided the champagne-popping, coke-sniffing lifestyle that all his drugs have no doubt sparked in others. His semi-detached home in a row of former council houses is run-down with a rusting old caravan sitting on the pavement outside. So where the hell is all his dosh?

The police remain convinced he's got it stashed away in a secret burial site or dotted around the world in foreign bank accounts. His girlfriend insisted he was broke after Andy's empire was exposed to the world when he was nicked in June 1999. But she would, wouldn't she?

Andy was caught in possession of 104kg of puff in his van which he'd just shipped in from Holland. It later turned out that one of his mates had grassed him up to the Old Bill. Detectives were told about a wooded area where more drugs were found plus £23,500 cash in his very tatty home. But there was no sign of the tens of millions of quid.

The beginning of the end for Andy came when his half-brother Tom McTaggart was nicked at Heathrow with £69,700 in cash, later found to be covered in traces of amphetamine and other drugs. A list of 'clients' was then found in McTaggart's house. He and Andy Billimore eventually came up with a great excuse; they reckoned the list was part of a Monopoly-style game called Skin-Up which they were devising together!

But even the cops said they were baffled by Andy's modest life in his £65,000 former council house in the village of Little Downham, Cambridgeshire. They produced evidence he was buying mountains of Charlie from Holland for £20,000 per kilogram and he'd even linked up with the Colombians for £16,000 per kilo. One of Andy's mates said he boasted he was importing 50 kilograms every three days.

One policeman explained, 'Drugs baron is the right word for him. He's a top league dealer. He'd had a few previous convictions. But successful drugs dealers don't get caught very often. That's why they're successful.'

In September 2000, Andy was sent down for 20 years when he admitted conspiracy to supply puff, supplying puff and plotting to pervert the course of justice. He was also found guilty of conspiring to supply Charlie. His half-brother, former paratrooper Tom McTaggert, also copped a long stretch following their two-week trial at Norwich Crown Court.

Andy was ordered to pay more than half a million quid within 12 months or face an extra four years on his sentence. As he sat in the dock, cuffed and surrounded by armed police, he shook his head when the fine was mentioned. Then Andy looked over to his live-in partner, sitting in the public gallery and motioned a telephone sign with his thumb and little finger. At the time of writing Andy still hasn't paid up the money. Naturally, his close friends and family insist he doesn't have the money. Andy claims to this day he was 'fitted up'.

The police think otherwise. 'He's one of the cleverest drug suppliers we've ever come across. He thought he'd never get nicked because he hid all his fortune so carefully, but we know he's one of the richest villains in Britain.'

CHAPTER
13

HITMAN JAKE

'The faces who hire me don't give a toss who I am. But I've got their respect. I do the job clean and simple with no fuckin' aggro.'

JAKE.

There's no shortage of work for a good hitman in today's Britain. The number of shootists on our streets has reached epidemic proportions. Twenty years ago, if you wanted someone bumped off there was only a small crew of highly professional killers-for-hire available. But in the year 2000, there were at least fifty rub-outs in Britain – and those are the ones the police know about.

Mind you, professional hits get little newspaper coverage. As old Fleet Street crime hack Peter Wilson says, 'One villain knocking off another doesn't have the same news appeal as a beautiful brunette blasting her cheating hubby to death.'

Hitmen themselves revel in the low-key nature of their business. Says one, 'The less publicity the better. The papers don't seem that interested in most hits.' Even the cozzers play down such crimes. As one detective explains, 'We take the attitude that every time there's a hit it means one less villain on the streets – and that can't be a bad thing.'

But now even the Met's finest admit the situation has grown completely out of control. They've set up a special squad to crack down on these so-called criminal renegades. David Veness, Assistant Commissioner in charge of specialist operations, admits, 'We have a genuine fear that there is a greater capacity for criminals to gain access to individuals willing to kill for money. There is clear evidence that there are small groups for whom this is the main form of criminal activity.' That's copspeak for: 'It's a big problem.'

The bottom line is that life's a lot cheaper in the 21st century than it was when sawn-off-shotgun-toting armed robbers swaggered across pavements taking pot shots at *The Sweeney*, as the plain clothes boys crouched behind their Ford Granadas. These days small-time hoods are prepared to knock off other villains, cheating lovers and work rivals. Some of the real pros are in danger of being put out of business.

Take my man Jake. He's been in 'the business' for twelve years, lives in a nice, comfortable three-bed bungalow in the Kent countryside, and no one other than his dear old mum, and his wife and kids knows his real identity. That's the way he intends to keep it. 'The fellows who hire me don't give a toss who I am. But I've got their respect. I do the job clean and simple with no fuckin' aggro,' explains Jake.

Jake reckons the hired hand who popped millionaire-gangster-turned-police-informant Pete McNeil, alias James Lawton, on 10 February 1998 didn't put a foot wrong. Coke-and-hooker addict McNeil, 40, was iced at point-blank range outside his very respectable, commuter-belt, redbrick modern detached home on the Bow Field housing estate in the twee Hampshire village of Hook. 'That was a classic hit,' says Jake. 'McNeil had it comin' for years.'

The victim had even been proudly telling people there was 'a bullet out there with my name on it' from the moment he turned supergrass when he was nicked for involvement in a $70 million coke heist. The drugs ring had links with an American branch of the Mafia in Detroit, not to mention a number of Medellin men from Colombia. So when McNeil finally got the bullet on his own doorstep at 8.01pm as a pot of pasta simmered on the stove, there wasn't a lot of grieving.

The list of suspects was longer than Michael Jordan's arm. There were criminal associates he'd double-crossed, ripped-off call girls, pissed-off coke dealers and even some poor mug who bought a second-hand car off McNeil and discovered it was a hot motor.

While no one can deny that Pete McNeil had it coming, there is no excuse for murder when hitmen shoot innocent people. That's what happened when little Dillon Hull, still clutching a toy, was hit twice in the head after a hired killer shot his 28-year-old stepdad John Bates in the stomach. Bates was a small-time smackhead/pusher on the lam from some big-time dope dealers in the unlikely setting of Bolton, Lancs. He was a recognised soldier in a vicious local drugs war while five-year-old Dillon was the innocent kid literally caught in the crossfire. Even hardened hitmen like my man Jake were gutted by the killing. 'It's fuckin' outrageous. Takin' a kid out like that. Makes me sick to think 'bout it.'

Within hours of the Dillon shooting, on 7 August 1997, the police were flooded with calls from local villains offering their services to help find the pratt who carried out probably the most cowardly hit ever witnessed on mainland Britain. 'There are too many fuckin' loose canons carryin' out hits in

exchange for a fix or a second-hand Fiesta. It's out of control …
and it's gonna get worse,' says one retired drug dealer from
south east London.

Back in June and July 1998, a posse of London Yardies
commissioned three barbaric murders, including the hitman-
style execution of two young mothers. The Met linked the
slayings after forensic tests revealed the victims were shot with
the same 9mm self-loading shooter. The posse plugged mums
Avril Johnson and Michelle Carby by shooting them in the
head at their own homes. The bodies were discovered by their
own kids.

The same Yardie firm rubbed out 34-year-old Patrick
Ferguson, inside his own home in Kingsbury, North London.
Each of the victims was linked to drug supply networks that
ran right across London from Brixton to Stratford, where
each of the women lived. The shootists were utterly ruthless;
they terrorised and sexually assaulted their victims in a
deliberate attempt to send a deadly message to their drug-
dealing rivals.

'This sorta thing might happen in Kingston, Jamaica, or
Cali, Colombia, even the east side of LA, but not London,
for fuck's sake,' says one old-time villain. 'It's completely
out of order.'

Gun violence spawned by the Yardie posses has escalated
dramatically in recent years. Of 160 murders in London in 1997,
41 victims were black and 18 of those were shot in classic Yardie-

style hits. To put this into prospective the black population of London only comprises 8% of the entire city.

Crack-smoking, Uzi-toting Yardies make the shootist who iced 57-year-old Great Train Robber Charlie Wilson by the pool of his 250 grand Marbella hacienda look like pussycats. 'It was a classic hit except that Wilson was a known face and that meant the police here and in Spain worked doubly hard to try and solve the case,' says one insider.

Wilson's killer was a pro called Billy Edmonds, 35. He rubbed Charlie out before freewheeling off, bizarrely, on a mountain bike. Not far down the hill he jumped into a motor driven by Danny 'Scarface' Roff – whose nickname came from the distinctive scar under his right eye and who had a fondness for chunky gold jewellery. At the time Scarface was on the run after escaping with Edmonds from a British nick while serving 13 years for armed robbery. Edmonds has been on the lam ever since.

Cops I know assure me that Wilson's murder, in April 1990, was commissioned on the orders of Londoner Roy Atkins who had been told Wilson had crossed him by allowing an arrested drug dealer to name him as a drug gang leader in return for a lighter sentence. Sounds like a case of dog eat dog. Atkins got his comeuppance when he took three bullets to the head while negotiating an E deal in an Amsterdam nighterie. Public enemy

Roff was re-arrested shortly afterwards as an escaped convict. But the Guardia Civil could never pin the Wilson job on him and the Dutch failed to nab him for the killing of Atkins, either.

So Roff was soon out of clink. In 1993 he took part in rubbing out another rival villain, property tycoon Donald Urquart. Urquart, 55, was shot three times in front of his girlfriend in Marylebone High Street, in central London. As one of Charlie Wilson's mates once told me, 'Trouble is, these things are never final. Each killing sparks more shootings which means a lot more faces will keep hitting the deck.'

Triggerman Scarface has since been linked to at least half a dozen other professional rub-outs. So it was hardly a surprise when he took his last breath on the driveway of his comfortable, mock-tudor detached mansion in Bromley, Kent, in March 1997. Already partly disabled from another failed attempt on his life, Scarface struggled out of his Mercedes 500SL into a wheelchair. At that moment the double doors of a rusting white Escort van parked a few yards away swung open and two fellows in black balaclavas and hoods opened fire. They hit Roff in the head and chest before burning rubber as the van's doors flapped while they careered away from the scene of the crime. They dumped the van half a mile down the road.

Life comes even cheaper if you mix it with the Triads. When they hit rival gang members it usually goes unreported – and unsolved – because of their Mafia-style secrecy and the fears of victims and witnesses. The four main societies – the 14K, We On Lok, Wo Shing Wo and San Yee On – rake in vast profits from protection rackets on restaurants and businesses, prostitution, fraud, illegal immigration and illicit gambling. That means there's plenty of work for their handpicked shootists.

One hit-man called Wai Hen Cheung, known as George in Soho, was even specially initiated into the Triads. George had to have his blood pricked from a finger into a glass of wine. Then he was instructed to join a gun club in Chingford, Essex, to learn how to handle lethal weapons. He was also given a job in a Chinese takeaway on the Channel Island of Guernsey so that his face would not be known around Soho while he was training up for his first hit. George later shot Hong Kong businessman Ying Kit Lam, 31, in a contract job intended to punish Lam and deter others from crossing the deadly Triads. But Lam lived, although he was crippled for life. George was sent down last year for a very long time.

Final word has to go to my man Jake, renowned as one of the most feared shootists on the streets of south east England. 'The rules of the game are changin' every day. My basic price is 20 grand, unless I'm bein' asked to take out a big-time face who's got a lot of protection. I always get paid in full, in advance, in cash. How else could I handle it, take a cheque? There are other unwritten clauses that go into every hit contract. If I get nicked the geezer commissioning the hit takes care of all my legal costs plus my bail if I manage to get it. He'd also make sure I was comfortable in the nick, that my missus was comfortable at home, as well as do everything to try and get me out. Finally, when I finished my bird, he would have a bundle of cash waiting for me. This is done to guarantee silence. As long as all obligations are taken care of, I'm not going to say a word to no one. I'm certainly not going to land anyone in the shit. They'd soon finish me off.'

But Jake says it's not the risk of being caught for his crimes that bothers him. 'There are other so-called pros out there poppin' people for five grand a piece. But you get what you pay for and these cut-price operators all get caught in the end and then they start singing. Let's face it, a granny in Blackpool who wants shot of her old man after thirty years of abuse is goin' to end up hiring a fuckin' amateur or an undercover cozzer.

'There's too many wideboys makin' out they can carry out hits for two and six. All they do is make problems for blokes like me.' But Jake reckons he has the answer. 'I'm plannin' to retire soon. Buy myself a nice little villa on the Costa Del Sol and start relaxin' and enjoyin' my life.' He pauses and nods his head slowly. 'If I live that long …'

CHAPTER 14

THE BRIEF –
MR HENRY MILNER

'Mr Milner's a real pro.
A complete gent. If you've got him
on side you're about 50% more likely
to walk out of court a free man.
He's a tasty operator.'

**ONE FORMER SOUTH EAST
LONDON BLAGGER.**

While Kenny Noye and a number of London's most feared faces like to keep understandably low profiles, the same cannot be said of their number one brief, Henry Milner. Since first representing Kenny during the Brink's-Mat investigation, 'Mr Milner' – as all his clients call him – has earned himself the respect of everyone from the most powerful faces to three of the suspects in the Stephen Lawrence murder.

And Mr Milner has no fears about the twilight world of the gangland criminals, many of whom pay top dollar for his services. He's not shy about saying how he's helped turn cases around even after his clients have been subjected to the old police habit of 'verballing up' suspects with false confessions. 'It's a lot of fun defending criminal cases,' admits Mr Milner.

Henry Milner's north London upbringing, Jewish boarding school education in Oxfordshire and degree at the London School of Economics couldn't be further removed from gangsterdom. At weekends, Mr Milner retreats even further from the London underworld with three hobbies: Tottenham Hotspur, bridge and traditional American music. But to his clients he remains the man they can trust to try and get them out of the tightest spots imaginable.

Legal eagle Henry Milner's one-man operation offers an exclusive service to ten or twelve rich clients a year. But Mr Milner does offer an entirely personal service. These days all his clients come through word of mouth. Mr Milner is a name that provokes a roll of the eyes and some sneaking admiration from just about every senior officer in the Met.

Mr Milner's small office is squeezed between two jewellery shops in the middle of the Adams Family's old stomping ground of London's Hatton Garden. His only employee, secretary Eileen, has worked for him for 23 years. Mr Milner's tiny waiting room has nothing but a handful of glossy mags to flick through. The lawyer's own office is panelled with dark oak and constantly filled with clouds of smoke from his ever-present fat Cuban cigars. They sit on his desk in a walnut veneer box crafted in a prison workshop and sent to him by a grateful client.

Mr Milner's first big professional breakthrough as a brief came in 1978 when he represented one of London's best-known 'faces' who, as Mr Milner later admitted, 'appeared at the Old Bailey as regularly as Frank Sinatra at the Albert Hall.' Mr Milner's 'lovable rogue' was eventually aquitted of criminal charges in six successive court cases. That was when word went out that Henry Milner was a brief to be trusted.

So when Brink's-Mat came round in 1983, Mr Milner was sitting pretty to receive a windfall of clients. First through the door was blagger Mickey McAvoy, followed by the legendary Tony White. Then came Kenny Noye. The list went on and on.

Mr Milner was once asked if there were any cases he wouldn't handle. He responded, 'That's a difficult question because I do a lot of cases the public finds distasteful, like drugs.

But I have never handled cases involving sexual offences on elderly people or young children.'

Luckily, Mr Milner says he's a born optimist. 'You've got to look confident even if you don't feel it,' he says. 'If you show a weakness or fear they will jump on it. Defendants are as shrewd as anything. They know whether you are on the ball.'

But even Mr Milner sometimes gets it wrong. One time he was representing an Iranian accused of possessing 100 kilos of heroin. Mr Milner was convinced the case was hopeless and that he'd be doing well if his client went down for less than 18 years. Mr Milner even begged the Iranian to plead guilty but he refused. The Iranian was aquitted and you get the impression Mr Milner still can't quite understand why.

Mr Milner insists he doesn't have a close relationship with any of his heavyweight clients, especially the superstar gangsters. He says he's never been out socialising with them apart from having the occasional sandwich at lunchtime.

One retired blagger told me recently, 'Mr Milner's a real pro. A complete gent. He doesn't have to hang around with the likes of us to understand the criminal mind. The guy's bloody brilliant. If you've got him on side you're about 50% more likely to walk out of court a free man. He's a tasty operator.'

Mr Milner prides himself on always having complete control of a case. That means deciding which witnesses to call, influencing a counsel's closing speech and occasionally putting his foot down. He's also renowned for picking top barristers with a knack for winning.

Not surprisingly, Mr Milner is well accustomed to the age-old question from many of his clients: 'What are my chances?' To his credit, he always gives them the straightest possible answer, although he did recently admit to one journalist: 'You start with "hopeless", "very, very poor", "under 50%", "evens" or "quite good". If you put it above "good", you're in trouble if they're found guilty.'

One of Mr Milner's favourites is: 'You can't guarantee anyone winning a case any more than love comes with a guarantee.'

Guarantee or no guarantee it seems that Henry Milner will remain the brief's name on most gangsters' lips for a long time to come.

THE SPECIALISTS

WENSLEY CLARKSON

THE FIXER

Immigration officer Guy Emmett has earned his place in this gangster hall of fame because without the 'fixers' of this world there would be no underworld. He's made a fortune from bribes by allowing illegal immigrants to stay in Britain as well as 'nodding through' a number of 'iffy'-looking passports being used by some of the most notorious faces on our streets today. As a passport officer at Gatwick Airport, Emmett was supposed to stop people illegally entering the country. Instead he started letting them in at a cost of up to £4,000 a time.

The scam enabled Emmett, on a modest salary of £20,000 a year, to live a millionaire's lifestyle. He splashed out on a £50,000 Porsche Carrera, a TVR sportscar, a BMW and a Lotus Elise. He bagged a total of seven properties, some of which were paid for with cash. In one eight-month period his bank accounts showed that Emmett was spending cash at a rate of £1,000 a day. While immigrants were his bread and butter, it was the fat cat criminals who made up his *crème de la crème*.

When Emmett was finally brought to justice, Home Office investigators only managed to trace 76 people allowed into the country illegally by Emmett. But they believed the true figure could be approaching 1,000.

Guy Emmett's criminal career took off shortly after he was posted to Gatwick's South Terminal in 1992 and continued for almost five years. Emmett ran the scam with 41-year-old immigration lawyer and adviser Christian Jideofo, himself an illegal immigrant from Nigeria who'd undergone a marriage of convenience in order to stay in Britain.

Soon Emmett was not only providing people with entry into this country, but was also stamping passports so they were given indefinite leave to remain and travel abroad, meaning they could come and go from Britain without any restrictions. He was a dream 'fixer' for many underworld figures who preferred to travel in and out of Britain on dodgy passports than allow the authorities to keep an eye on their movements.

As prosecutor Mark Gadsen explained at Emmett's Old Bailey trial, 'He systematically endorsed passports of foreigners who had no right to remain here with stamps that would be accepted by the authorities and give them the right to stay here.'

Emmett used his own official stamp and that of a colleague to endorse the passports. In 1993 he even set up his own immigration advisory business, called Stephen Goodfellows, in Thornton Heath, Surrey, even though that was strictly against the terms of his employment. Soon word got out that he was an immigration officer with few scruples if the price was right.

His mate, Jideofo, who operated from offices in Kilburn, north west London, sent his 'clients' to Emmett. Jideofo also sent passports to Emmett, who would enter official stamps. Clients paid deposits of up to £2,000 beforehand plus the balance on receipt of the stamped passports.

Those official stamps also smoothed the path to British citizenship for at least 50% of his 'customers' by indicating the passport holders had been checked out and deemed suitable for residency. Jideofo also arranged for bogus letters purporting to show the holders had been allowed UK residency.

'Clients' were even provided with a crib sheet of what to say if they were challenged at a port of entry. Their details had all been entered on the Home Office computer and they were told to tell any suspicious official, 'Check my passport with the computer.' Their written instructions finished by stating, 'Don't panic, don't change your story and everything will be all right.'

Guy Emmett's reign as the passport king of Gatwick only came to an end when a suspicious solicitor contacted the chief immigration officer. Emmett was arrested the following year, in June 1996, but not charged until 1999. He steadfastly insisted that although the stamps in the passports were bogus he was not the culprit.

Emmett, of Furze Lane, Purley, Surrey, and Jideofo, of Kingston Road, New Barnet, Hertfordshire, were convicted of conspiring to defraud the Home Secretary and assist illegal immigrants to enter the UK. Emmett's wife Elizabeth, 30, also an immigration officer at Gatwick, was cleared of any involvement on the direction of the judge halfway through the six-week trial. A third man, Sam Essuah, who gave evidence for the prosecution, had earlier been jailed for 12 months in 1998 after admitting four immigration offences. He introduced many paying customers to Emmett.

Guy Emmett was eventually sentenced to eight years in prison. Judge Timothy Pontius told the 35-year-old villain that his greed had led him 'without regret or shame to betray the high standards of integrity and trust' expected of immigration officials. His partner Jideofo got a six-and-a-half-year stretch.

But it wasn't all bad new for fixer Guy Emmett. The police reckon he's got a small fortune stashed away in the Channel Isles. And no doubt he'll be dabbling in some stocks and shares while he's watching the daisies grow from his cell window.

THE SUPERGRASS

No book about gangsters in the 21st century would be complete without a look inside the world of the 'supergrass'. Without informants, it's highly unlikely that any gangsters would ever be apprehended.

Computer nerd Martin Grant was recruited from inside Blantyre House open prison in Kent to help a bunch of notorious gangsters, including Kenny Noye and John 'Little Legs' Lloyd, set up a credit card scam they believed could net them tens of millions of pounds. Grant – jailed for attempting to murder his wife and child – had studied for a degree in electronic communications while in the slammer.

Eventually, he was allowed out of prison on a day-release programme for work experience at a van hire business owned by Paul Kidd, another villain involved with Noye and Lloyd's cashcard cloning scheme. The gang planned to enter British Telecom exchanges with a team of corrupt engineers to put telephone taps on the lines and memory boards. This information was then to be transferred to the gang's computer.

In mid-summer of 1995, the gang enjoyed a champagne dinner at a Kent hotel. Six prostitutes were then hired for £3,000 for the entire night to service all the crooks. Amongst the villains was nerdy computer wizard Martin Grant. Unknown to the gang, Grant – who was plainly out of his depth amongst this team of veritable hardmen – was already feeding information about the credit card scam to police. He'd earlier confessed to a prison chaplain about the planned robbery before making a statement of over 300 pages to Scotland Yard detectives.

Grant got cold feet that evening because he didn't want to sleep with any hookers, let alone the ones specially recruited in London's West End by Kenny Noye. Noye was infuriated and only agreed to keep Grant on the team because his computer knowledge was invaluable.

Grant was doubly nervous because he knew he was a dead man if any of the gang found out he was double-crossing them. Eventually, he forced himself to sleep with one girl in case it gave him away. It was a disaster and the other gang members made fun of him because of his failure to perform.

On 25 July 1995, police raided a farmhouse in Yalding, Kent, and seized more than 70,000 blank cashcards plus 28 computer disks. A murder contract was immediately put out on computer boffin-turned-supergrass Martin Grant. Noye and the rest of the gang knew he'd stitched them up. 'The word went out that certain faces were prepared to pay double the going rate [£20,000] to get Grant plugged,' one retired villain later recalled.

As Roy Ramm, one of the senior detectives involved in the case, later explained, 'The scam was a classic example of a group of South London robbers and villains who saw an opportunity to get a great deal of money, but did not have the technical expertise so they worked outside their circle and brought in somebody [Grant] who eventually destroyed them.'

Some years later, Martin Grant came out of hiding to reveal what it felt like to double-cross so-called master criminals Kenny Noye and John 'Little Legs' Lloyd. 'They were just names to me at first. They meant nothing. But people inside Blantyre House talked about them as if they were gods,' he recalled.

Grant insists he tried to walk away from the scam. 'I said I thought it wouldn't work. But another inmate told me if I wasn't careful I'd lose my eye. That's when I contacted the police.'

Grant said he attended one meeting with the gang where Noye produced prison paperwork on his (Grant's) record and family background which clearly had been given to Noye by prison staff. Those details included the addresses of Grant's mother and brother.

Then, in a chilling incident, John 'Little Legs' Lloyd drove Grant up to his mother's house and walked him through the front door, even introducing himself to Grant's mother, 'just to let me know he knew where she lived'. Grant added, 'John Lloyd then phoned Kenny Noye to say he had met my mum. I was so scared.' Grant says that when he decided to go to the police about the scam he was too terrified to report anything to staff at Blantyre House'.

Grant says that Noye became very threatening towards him once he and Lloyd began suspecting he might have grassed on them. 'One time they got a bunch of other villains to follow me back to prison to make sure I wasn't in touch with the police,' he said.

Grant claimed that while still in Blantyre House he was handed £50,000 by an inmate who was given it by a visitor who was a contact of Kenny Noye's. The cash was supposed to secure Grant's role in the scam, but instead he claims he threw it away in disgust. 'I didn't want the money but it shows just how powerful Kenny Noye was that he could get that money to me inside jail,' said Grant.

Then Noye even opened a building society account in

Grant's name and started dropping small amounts of cash into it. The gangsters were trying to lock Grant in so he could not back out of the scam or dare to grass them up. They knew he was the weakest link.

Hours before the arrest of the Hole-in-the-Wall suspects including Lloyd (Noye was never charged in connection with the crime even though he was later named in open court), Martin Grant was placed in police custody 'for his own protection'. Detectives put him in a safe house with armed officers 24 hours a day and only moved him by helicopter.

Grant concluded, 'I know they hold a grudge against me and I'm very nervous about it. Remember, I have seen the other side of Kenny Noye not so much against me but against others who have mucked him about. Although he can be a very nice chap he is quite capable of turning into an aggressor.'

Grant had absolutely no idea what he was letting himself in for when he signed up for the witness protection programme. There are two distinct catagories of protected witnesses. The first is the innocent bystander. If they agree they are given every privilege imaginable and helped to set up a new life. The second category are professional criminals like Martin Grant who turn grass because it is their only choice if they want to avoid more prison sentences.

And the police never let people like Grant forget they are criminals. Rather than being kept in a hotel or safe house, they spend their time being moved between special secure units and police stations. As Grant later said, 'It was worse than the open prison I was already in.'

At the time of writing, Martin Grant was still in hiding, afraid that Kenny Noye and his associates wish to do him harm. His only clue about where he resided was to say, 'It's somewhere north of Watford ...'

THE GUNSMITH

Gangsters are involved in so many heavyweight scenes these days that most of them are tooled up at all times. That means there is a small, select band of armourers – better known as gunsmiths – on duty 24 hours a day.

Ex-Met police officer Sidney Wink was gunsmith numero uno, at the top of his tree. He had the respect and ear of many of London's most fearsome gangsters despite having once been Old Bill. 'But then he had to have some bottle with that background, didn't he?' one old face recently remarked.

Wink's speciality, although never proved in a court of law, was renumbering illegal weapons, including those used by members of the Brink's-Mat gang. (It never ceases to amaze how much of this book connects to Brink's-Mat.)

Sid Wink was also strongly suspected of supplying the guns used in two murders – the 1992 contract killing of Kenny Noye's

London money launderer Donald Urquart, and the shooting of PC Patrick Dunne by three Yardie gunmen.

Not surprisingly, Wink's background as a cop made the police even more infuriated by his very existence. As one retired thief taker told me, 'Wink was the pits. A man who had represented law and order only to go across to the other side and even supply a weapon that was used in the shooting of a policeman. He was a bloody disgrace.'

But being a gunsmith is no picnic. Wink found himself dealing with some of the most deadly criminals in Britain, which meant he always had to be on his guard. 'Some of them didn't trust him at first because of his background. You could say Sid overcame more obstacles than most criminals,' says one former police colleague.

By the early Nineties, Sid Wink was starting to feel the pressure that inevitably accompanied such a deadly career move. He was renowned for supplying untraceable weapons, but some villains thought he'd been ripping them off by charging high prices for weapons, so they decided to have a word in the ear of the local constabulary.

'That's when Sid started getting visits from the cozzers at all times of the day and night. He started to get really freaked out and tried to slow down his operation so he was only supplying villains he knew and trusted,' explained one former face.

But in August 1994, a week after officers investigating PC Dunne's murder raided his Essex home, the pressure got too much for old Sid Wink. He put a pistol to his head and pulled the trigger, taking a lot of very tasty secrets with him to his grave.

May the Lord have mercy on his soul ...

CONCLUSION

Yes, crime really is this country's third biggest industry. It's not an easy concept to handle, is it? Gangsters bring more cash into this country than almost anyone else. And when they spend it, they often help keep legit businesses afloat, especially in tough inner city areas like Liverpool and Manchester.

The sad truth is that the police aren't going to make much difference. If they can lay their hands on 10% of the proceeds, they're doing well. These days drugs, arms dealing, racketeering and even murder bring in more cash than the old favourites like security van blaggings.

People don't seem to have a clue that the UK is in the grip of organised crime. Most law-abiding citizens think drug dealers are a bunch of scruffy geezers hanging out on street corners flogging crack. Truth is, those sort of vermin are at the lowest level of criminality, although it's true to say a lot of them work for the big boys who live in the detached mansions, drive the flashy motors and send their kids to public schools.

Perhaps the most scary thing is that those drugs are fuelling so many of the shootings on our streets today. The underworld is a powerful and deadly place. No doubt about it.

Back in 2000 a gunman let rip at dozens of innocent people lining up outside a London nightclub in the early hours of the morning, injuring nine people, including a 16-year-old kid. The attack – at Chicago's in Peckham – was blamed on Yardie gangsters and it didn't even get a mention on the TV news the following day. These sort of random gangland shoot-outs are two a penny in Britain nowadays. And many of the faces mentioned in this book thrive on the fear provoked by such attacks.

The statistics speak for themselves. At least 100 murders a year can be linked to organised crime. And hundreds more victims are hurt in shootings like the one in Peckham. Then there are the gangsters chopped into little pieces by their enemies who disappear without trace.

Sure, there's nothing new about gangsters living alongside us. But, say many of the old school villains, in the past ten years the situation has got completely out of control. Some of the younger, under-40, gangsters are threatening the peace and stability that the older faces helped promote.

Today, there are four main groups of organised crime. The British families and certain other big-time operators are well-known to the law and many of them – as you will have already read here – have been in and out of the slammer half their lives. Drugs and the illegal booze 'n' fags trade seem to be their main 'businesses'.

Then come the foreigners and more specifically what the Old Bill call the 'Turkish Groups', mostly Cypriots but including a lot of Kurds. And I can tell you that the Kurds are a bunch of mad bastards. This group is reckoned to be behind more than 90% of this country's importation of heroin, the highest in Europe. These characters are pure evil.

Then there's the third group, the Chinese 'snakehead' gangs; groups of gangsters so secretive that I couldn't dig deep enough into their backgrounds to provide a chapter on any of them. They stick together, dabbling in drugs and protection rackets mainly within their own Chinese communities. The latest mainstay of their income is from the activity exposed by the death of 50 Chinese illegal immigrants in a lorry at Dover in the middle of 2000. The trade in people with up to £10,000 charged per person for their clandestine trips to the UK, is taking over from drugs as their most lucrative enterprise.

Then comes the fourth – and definitely most deadly group – the Yardies. These nutters are mainly of Jamaican origin, but during the 90s they've come out on to the streets of our cities armed to the teeth. The Yardies have all but sewn up the crack cocaine market. But to get together the huge amounts of cash needed to purchase drug shipments they're not averse to some racketeering, protection and gun trading.

And let me assure you that the Yardies even strike fear into many of the gangsters whose stories feature in this book. This lot think nothing of topping each other if they have a ruck. Anyone outside their tightly knit team who crosses them will almost certainly pay for it with their life. The Uzi-toting Yardies operate by a different set of rules from everyone else. The police are really struggling to contain them on certain manors in the big cities.

The Yardies were linked to the shooting at the Chicago club in Peckham which I mentioned earlier. It could have been a revenge attack, but it's more likely a protecton issue designed to terrify the manor and gain even bigger helpings of respect from the community. In many ways, these British Yardies are copying the street soldiers in US cities like LA and New York. Over in the Big Apple, one of the most deadly gangs is called the Shower People because they like showering people with bullets and they don't give a toss who gets caught in the crossfire.

Many of the megawealthy, more low-key gangsters featured in this book are just as concerned by the Yardies as the rest of us. 'Most of us just want to get on with our businesses but these nutters are attracting attention and that's bad news for the rest of us. It's also well out of order to hit innocent women and children. The rest of us just wouldn't do that sorta thing,' says one old London face.

Naturally the cops would love to see us introduce Zero Tolerance like they have on the streets of New York in order to crack down on all sorts of crimes. But what they don't seem to realise is that a lot of these Yardies were driven over here from the US because of that very policy. I've been told that more than a dozen of New York and LA's most fearsome street gang members are operating in our cities as we speak. They don't give a toss who gets in their way. Reputations mean nothing. It's rumoured that three of these nutters have got a price on their heads because some of the old school gangsters want them out of the way. 'They're nothin' but trouble. It makes good financial sense to have a whip round and have these sorta bastards taken out,' says one old-timer.

Only recently American gangster Olatunde Adetoro was jailed for life after a crazy gun-toting rampage through Lancashire and Greater Manchester. He tried to shoot his way out of police custody with an AK-47 assault rifle and even snatched an innocent bystander. This new generation of psycho-gangsters would shoot their own grannies dead over a drug deal. No wonder the Old Bill are struggling to get to grips with the problem. But it's not helped by the massive wall of silence from the faces in the thick of things.

Everything's stacked against the Old Bill. No witnesses ever come forward. The cops recently set up Operation Trident, an intelligence-gathering operation investigating shootings by blacks against other blacks. It stands more chance of smoking out the psychos than anything else. Now every single Yardie incident is handled at a central bureau where the MO of each crime is carefully monitored. MI5, the National Criminal Intelligence Bureau and police across the nation all pool their information. But the truth is it's only going to scratch the surface.

What the big-time, multi-millionaire gangsters like the ones featured in this book really fear is the setting up of an FBI-type organisation which would bring together all the agencies fighting against organised crime. The older faces have become so worried they've even been trying to buy up politicians on both sides to make sure that any legislation does not get through.

Meanwhile, the streets of Britain continue to be run by rich and powerful gangsters. But what of the future? Will all the old faces survive? And who's trying to muscle into this nation's underworld as we speak?

The Nigerian Mafia is a classic example. Britain's become a key staging post for teams of African smugglers dealing in everything from people to smack. Until recently the Nigerians concentrated on complex frauds and benefit scams, but now they've started investing their dirty money in the biggest earner of all – heroin. In Chicago, for example, the Nigerians already control 90% of the smack trade.

The police are so freaked out by the Nigerians that both the Customs and Excise and the National Criminal Intelligence Service (NCIS) have set up specialist squads to monitor and infiltrate the West African organised crime members slipping into Britain. They've got agents circling the globe trying to keep up with the movements of these frightening firms of psycho-criminals.

But the Russians are way in front of the Nigerians. Many of the top Mafia bosses from the former Soviet Union have been secretly buying into legitimate firms and splashing out on massive properties here in order to get a toehold in Britain. 'The

Russian villains are buying up houses in areas like Pinner in West London because it's so handy for Heathrow. We've become like a staging post to a lot of very active gangsters,' explained one British hood who's worked with the Russians in Britain.

One of the world's top criminals, Sergei Mikhailov, is already being linked to a number of British gangsters. Mikhailov was based in Moscow until recently. As one retired London face told me, 'Being British doesn't mean anything any more. These characters come from all over the world and see that we've got a few bob here and they want a piece of the action. It's as simple as that.' And he warned, 'There's going to be even more killings on the streets because these foreigners don't give a toss about innocent passersby. If you cross them you're dead. Bang. Bang.'